More by
KEMALA B. TRIBE

The Head-Smacker Series

Disarming Deadly Doctrines – Stop Sickness in its Tracks
with Head-Smacking Revelations of God's Will
available at kemalatribe.com, MyStore.com, Amazon

Debunking Deceptive Doctrines (working title – upcoming)

Doctrines of Demons (working title – upcoming)

Shorts

"Summer Breeze"
Awarded publication in
"Southern Writers Best
Short Fiction 2015"
Available on Amazon

"Daddy Knows"
Published in Chicken
Soup for the Soul's
"Dreams and the Unexplainable"
Available whereever books are sold

"Picking Presents"
A 6-year-old's Christmas life lesson
to read every holiday season
Available on Amazon

"Storming Tara"
Very short romance
Available on Amazon

"The Definition of Seafaring"
Love & danger on the high seas
Available on Amazon

Freebies @ kemalatribe.com

To download gifts
such as these, go to
kemalatribe.com and
join my mailing list.

{
Printable Confession Cards
List of Healing Scriptures
Healing Action Plan
Books by Guest Authors
Inspiring Short Stories
And more (will vary, visit often)
}

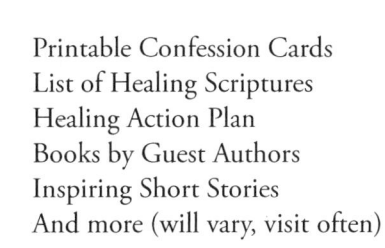

You will receive one or two articles per month chock full of head-smacking revelations from my Be Positive blog. I promise I won't clog your inbox.

Contact the author using the form at kemalatribe.com

How Many Miracles is One Person Allowed?

Retitled 2nd Ed.
of *Everyday, God.*
plus
5 more miracles!

Extraordinary Accounts
from an Ordinary Christian

Kemala B. Tribe

Copyright © 2021, 2024 by Kemala B. Tribe

All rights reserved. No part of this book may be reproduced or transmitted in any form or by any means, electronic or mechanical, including photocopying, recording, or by any information storage and retrieval system without the written permission of the author, except where permitted by law.

ISBN 979-8-9897601-0-7 paperback
ISBN 979-8-9897601-2-1 hardcover
ISBN 979-8-9897601-1-4 ebook
ISBN 979-8-9897601-3-8 large print

Edited by Jan Youmans Mason
Interior Design by Eleuteria A. Wenceslao
Cover Design by Kemala B. Tribe

Image on front cover by Harryarts from Freepik.com

Published in the USA by

WingShadow Publishing

Milton, Florida

For my son
— himself the most wonderful of miracles —
who, though often unaware,
was integral to the
narratives herein.

TABLE OF CONTENTS

Chapter 1	MIRACLES More Than You Can Ask or Think	1
Chapter 2	OVERRULING THE LAWS OF NATURE Moving Heaven and Earth	7
Chapter 3	PROTECTION Guardian Angels - Your Own Secret Service	35
Chapter 4	HEALINGS It's All About Freedom	53
Chapter 5	PROVISION Feeding the Flock	83
Chapter 6	RELATIONSHIPS Remaining in Love	103
Chapter 7	BINDING UP THE BROKEN HEARTS Nobody Knows but Jesus	109
Chapter 8	INEXPLICABLE HAPPENINGS There's No Such Thing as Coincidence	119
Chapter 9	MIRACLES JUST FOR YOU Expect Them, Receive Them	141

GLOSSARY OF BIBLE TRANSLATIONS　　　　　　　　　147

- 1 -

MIRACLES
More Than You Can Ask or Think

What do you need today? God will provide it.

Yes, it's that simple. This book is not just a collection of testimonies. It's not just an anthology of short (true) stories for bedtime reading. It's not just a morning devotional. It's proof that God's promises are real and are for you. It's a reference book of God's power constantly at work in all realms of earthly existence today.

Why would God do so much for just one person? Because I am His child. Are you His child? Then take this book as proof that He'll do the same for you — everyday. After all, what wouldn't you do for your child?

Believe me, there is nothing special about me. I've sinned just as much as you, possibly more. I mess up every day in one way or another. Yet God shows off in my life on a regular basis. If you're not constantly seeing His grace and His power in action, then the only difference between us is likely that I EXPECT Him to do whatever it takes to care for me every day. Regardless of what my need is, I trust Him to meet it. I do not trust myself to take care of myself — at least, I try not to. With this book I hope to inspire you to trust Him more and expect more from Him. Expectation is the highest form of faith, and He will honor it even if it requires overriding the laws of physics.

Yes, the miraculous is found in the natural — the architecture of a nautilus shell, conception, how daisy petals curl up before it rains, the flight of bumblebees. But that is not what this book is about. It's about receiving obvious and indisputable miracles of protection, health, provision and blessings of all kinds as you go about your everyday life. God will turn that life — your life — into an action-adventure story. People will speak of you to others, "You won't believe what happened to this guy I met the other day…," and God will be glorified.

—&—

Protection, health and provision — would you bear with me while I expound a bit, before we get to the amazing accounts I want to share with you? These are the three main areas where we need hope in this crazy time. So many of us think of the Promises as things we have to look forward to in heaven, but I hope the experiences I've chronicled here will prove that theory wrong for you. God keeps His Promises, whatever it takes, when you believe. If that means doing something so grand that we call it a miracle, so be it.

Protection is a promise of God:

> For he will give his angels orders concerning you, to protect you in all your ways.
> - Psalm 91:11 CSB

We won't need protection when we're in heaven. All the danger is here; all the sickness is here; all the persecution is here; all the demons are here. None of these things can harass us in heaven. Without God's protection, the enemy would take you out of the game, and the Lord would lose a laborer. Protection is for here and now.

Health is a promise of God:

> My son, give attention to my words; incline your ear to my sayings. Do not let them depart from your sight; keep them in the midst of your heart. For they are life to those who find them and health to all their body.
> - Proverbs 4:20-23 NASB

Health allows you to carry out God's work at peak efficiency. Why would you need healing in heaven when you're going to leave your body here? The scripture you just read says the Word is health to your *body*. Some translations say *flesh*. Our glorified bodies in heaven won't be made of corruptible flesh. Healing is for here and now.

Provision is a promise of God:

> The Lord is my shepherd, I shall not want.
> - Psalm 23:1

Biblical provision and prosperity apply to all areas of life, not just finances. However, the financial aspect is the one Christians often get hung up on, and ironically, need most, from all appearances. I've learned, as you'll glean from these pages, to lean on God for provision, not my late husband and certainly not myself. God's economy doesn't work the way the world's works. The world cannot feed five thousand families with one boy's lunch. The Lord does multiplication miracles for tithers all the time. And the stress reduction in handing the weight of responsibility for bringing home the bacon off to the Lord — it's life-altering. Some seem to fear that by accepting God's financial prosperity here, we'll have less in our heavenly account for eternity in heaven. You won't need it there. It's a tool for living life in this world and spreading the gospel. Provision is for here and now.

—&—

What about the issue of feeling selfish when you ask God for blessings? It's not ONLY for you, you know. He blesses us to be a blessing. The more He pours into you, the more you can pour out to others. He is blessed when you receive from Him because it is His nature to give. And He is blessed when you give to others because He wants to see His nature revealed to others through you. You are, after all, made in His image.

Whether it's testimonies, finances, encouragement, assistance, or friendship, you have more to give when you've received from God.

> And God is able to make all grace [every favor and earthly blessing] come in abundance to you, so that you may always [under all circumstances, regardless of the need] have complete sufficiency in everything [being completely self-sufficient in Him], and have an abundance for every good work *and* act of charity.
> - 2 Corinthians 9:8 AMP

Isn't that a great phrase — self-sufficient in Him? He LOVES to pour out His grace and blessings on us, meeting our needs and beyond. Remember 3 John 1:2, "...be in health and prosper, even as your soul prospers"? He wants us to have the things we want as long as those things don't HAVE US. Let Him be God! You can never put a dent in His supply, nor reduce the gifts He has available for others. So receive everything He wants to give you, and what He wants to give you includes the things you want to ask for. If you don't, you're telling Him, "No. I don't want what You're offering," — not really the best posture before the Almighty.

Do you wonder if you're worthy of receiving His blessings? God is so intent on blessing and protecting His children, that even pre-Jesus, when there was no true remission of sin, He constantly blessed His people. Balaam said,

> Behold, I have received *a command* to bless;
> He has blessed, and I cannot reverse it.
> - Numbers 23:20 KJV

He has blessed, and we cannot reverse that. Jesus later provided it all in His substitutionary suffering — it's already done. And He qualified us when He made us righteous. So those blessings are going out to the world, and you only have to believe they're for you to receive them. There's no crown in heaven for refusing what God has already provided for you. No, it is His nature to give good gifts to His children, and He is our model for good parenting.

So don't be shy about receiving the miracles of His promises. As He told one pastor that I listen to, He gives more than anyone else gives. Since it's more blessed to give than to receive, He still gets the better end of the deal!

— & —

My husband was very good at his job. He was a ship's captain, and later he worked in very technical shore-based positions and as a consultant in the marine industry. He did everything with excellence. When he told me about a problem solved, a promotion earned, a new achievement, a brilliant idea, or a bonus received, I rarely got excited. I simply said something like, "I wouldn't expect anything less." It was my smile as I said it that made him know he was greatly appreciated. He would glow in that low-key applause, knowing it was high praise. I expected him to excel at every turn, and he never disappointed. I made sure he felt appreciated, and he always knew I had confidence in him.

I'm the same with God in that I expect great things, and He delivers. Therefore, I have a grateful heart toward Him constantly. I remind myself often of how He loves me and has always looked out for me, and that keeps me in faith. I praise Him not only because I'm truly thankful, but also because it's effective warfare against the enemy. I'm ever-so-grateful on the heart level, and I brag on Him every chance I get. There's the difference between how I responded to my husband and how I respond to God. It was not important that others knew how great my husband was, but it's essential others know how great my God is in my life. It may influence where they spend eternity. So welcome to my book.

— & —

These testimonies are very personal, some were gut-wrenching to write and even more so to publish. From that perspective, I'd rather not share them. But it is necessary to give the context in order to understand the blessing. And so I am baring my soul in some of these accounts, and exposing my questionable past. I considered changing every name but my own in the interest of the privacy of others. Then I realized it wouldn't disguise anyone's identity from those who know me, and I've told most of them about these occurrences, anyway. And to those who will never meet me or my family, what will it matter? So to you who have been part of my blessed life so far, I thank you, and credit you and the Lord with the blessing these testimonies will be to others.

Now let me say, not every supernatural act should technically be called a miracle. But if something happens because you apply scriptural principles, such as tithing, or a person is supernaturally protected because they take God at His word and read Psalm 91 regularly, does that make it any less a miracle? I don't think so. Healings are just the speeding up of the natural healing process — not technically a miracle…unless a new limb or organ is grown — that's called a creative miracle. I'm labeling them all as miracles in this book, though, for the sake of simplicity.

A miracle is really just an answer to somebody's prayer — perhaps a bit more grandiose than other answers. In other words, a miracle is a way of meeting a need. One could say that if we're living by God's principles, we should seldom need a miracle. And it's true that we shouldn't need to live from miracle to miracle, healing to healing — we should be walking in His benefits, daily. But at the same time, as you will see here, when you walk in faith, God does whatever it takes to prove His Word true, answer that prayer, make His promises manifest, provide what you have faith in Him for, and shower you with His love. Sometimes it's so amazing that we get to point to it and say, "It's a miracle!"

As I prepare this book for your reading, I feel the Holy Spirit is on the edge of His seat with anticipation. That tells me that some of you will receive your miracle through the inspiration these testimonies provide. Let one of those recipients be YOU.

– 2 –

OVERRULING THE LAWS OF NATURE
Moving Heaven and Earth

> A scientist who would know the laws of nature must sit passively before nature. He may not dictate to nature its laws, nor may he impose his own intelligence upon nature; rather, the more passive he is before nature, the more nature will reveal its secrets.
> - Fulton J. Sheen

> A miracle is not the suspension of natural law, but the operation of a higher law.
> - Unknown

Proof of God's Will

> "Behold, the virgin shall be with child...
> - Matthew 1:23 NKJV

> Then Moses stretched out his hand over the sea. The Lord drove the sea back with a powerful east wind all that night and turned the sea into dry land...
> - Exodus 14:21-22 CSB

...the master of the banquet tasted the water that had been turned into wine... "you have saved the best till now."

- John 2:1-11 NIV

"Sun, stand still over Gibeon, and moon, over the Valley of Aijalon. "And the sun stood still and the moon stopped until the nation took vengeance on its enemies.

- Joshua 10:13-14 CSB

Therefore, if anyone is in Christ, he is a new creation; the old has passed away, and see, the new has come!

- 2 Corinthians 5:17 CSB

And Peter got out of the boat, and walked on the water and came toward Jesus.

- Matthew 14:29 NASB

...Only the fleece was dry, and dew covered the ground.

- Judges 6:36-40 ESV

But do not overlook this one fact, beloved, that with the Lord one day is as a thousand years, and a thousand years as one day.

- 2 Peter 3:8 ESV

And the LORD was going before them in a pillar of cloud by day to lead them on the way, and in a pillar of fire by night to give them light, so that they might travel by day and by night.

- Exodus 13:21 NASB

CHEMISTRY LESSON

Chief Officers have the most difficult job on any ship, but particularly on a chemical tanker. Our tanker had fifty-two tanks. Theoretically, that meant you could carry fifty-two different cargoes with fifty-two different sets of requirements. It's a complex puzzle that must be solved for every port visited and every cargo loaded.

Some tanks were stainless steel, some were heated, some were refrigerated, some were polyurethane-coated, some were above deck, and some were below deck. Some cargoes required nitrogen to be pumped in before loading because they couldn't be exposed to oxygen without explosive results; some would cause an explosion that would take out half a city if one drop of seawater got in; others might have the same effect if one drop of the chemical went into the harbor. Many of them couldn't be mixed with specific other chemicals without vaporizing the ship. Part of the Chief Officer's responsibilities is to make sure that doesn't happen.

One way he does that is to keep a record of the last five cargoes in every tank, in order to eliminate any risk of a residual bit of those cargoes making contact with another chemical it doesn't play well with. Cleaning these cargo tanks is another essential part of the puzzle. Each type of cargo has specific cleaning agents (more chemicals) that can or cannot be used.

After a cargo is pumped ashore, the crew cleans the empty tank. That means dropping cleaning machines down into a tank, hooking them up to hot water and/or the correct cleaning agents for that cargo, and turning them on to do their job. But for many cargoes the cleaning machines are not thorough enough.

How much more cleaning is required is determined by the outcome of a lab test, called a wall wash, performed by the Chief Officer or by the Bosun at the Chief's request. The bosun climbs down into the tank once it's been cleared as safe (no toxic fumes) with a squirt bottle of distilled water, acetone or methanol and a stainless steel tool that looks a lot like a squeegee with a funnel attached. He squirts the liquid onto the tank wall and allows it to run down the wall a ways before catching it with the funnel. He then takes the liquid to the chemistry lab attached to the Chief's office and tests it for residual traces of the last cargo. This level of cleanliness is measured in parts per million (ppm) of residue. The ppm of the last cargo's residue dictates whether or not the tank is ready to receive the next load based on exactly what that next cargo is to be, because the tolerance of residue for each cargo varies. Simple right?

Well, not always. Sometimes you have a tank whose last two cargoes were not quite compatible — not anything dangerous to mix, but perhaps not good for the tank itself. The two cargoes could combine to cause a film on the tank walls that is very hard to remove, or it could pit the stainless steel or whatever material a certain tank is coated with. This can cause real problems, both for the crew who has to get that tank clean somehow and for the shipping company because of costly delays.

How do I know all this? I sailed for years with my husband on chemical tankers. I went ashore when I got pregnant, and then we all sailed together once our son was walking and talking well.

Around the time the baby turned two and we hadn't joined my husband yet on his ship, the phone rang late one night, and I picked it up on the kitchen extension. It was my husband, phoning from the ship, sounding exhausted and ever-so frustrated.

"…And they're down in there again now. They're exhausted. You can't imagine how hot it is in the tank. "

"But why's this particular tank so hard to clean?"

"I don't know. Well, for one thing, the tank coating is pitted. We washed it first with hot water, then with Cleaner B. That didn't work so we used B again. Then I sent the men in to clean by hand, and the test still came back high. So we used C, which we really weren't supposed to use, and it still tested high. So the men went in again, but we still got bad results."

"Well, what are your tolerances? How many ppm is acceptable?"

"Zero."

"ZERO?"

"Yeah, we're scheduled to load methanol, and being a solvent, you have to prove 0 ppm or you're not loading."

"So what are you going to do?"

"Well, we've run another machine wash with C, and the men are using scrub brushes one last time. If the wall wash doesn't pass this time, we don't have any choice — we're going to have to leave the dock, go to the anchorage, and the men are going to have to go back in and chip the entire coating off the inside of the tank by hand. Then we'll have to have it recoated. There's no telling how long that process will take, and it's going to cost hundreds of thousands of dollars in lost time and revenue, plus the cost of labor and recoat, not to mention the office will have to find alternative carriers for the cargoes we're already contracted for. It'll be a real mess. And the time delay — I don't know if we'll be back in port for crew change, so I might not even be home on time. Management is gonna blow a gasket, so I'll have them breathing down my neck, too. Like I need more pressure. You know what it's like on the Gulf Coast — I'm so busy I don't know if I'm coming or going. The only sleep I've gotten in the last thirty-six hours has been naps at my desk. "

"Well, honey, have you prayed about it?"

"What?"

"Have you prayed? Over the tank?"

"Uh…no. Honestly, I hadn't even thought of it."

"So, when will Mr. Tria and the guys be finished in the tank and do the next wall-wash?"

"Within the hour."

"So if the test comes back high again, before you give up, go pray over the tank, OK? God doesn't want you to have all these hassles or to be delayed coming home. He doesn't want you under this much stress. I'll bet He's just itching for you to ask Him for help."

"Yeah… Yeah, you're right! Good plan — I'm gonna pray over it. I'm almost hoping the tank DOESN'T test clean so God can show up and show off."

Ninety minutes later I got the rest of the story.

"It didn't work — the scrub brushes, I mean. The guys came in looking like they could hardly put one foot in front of the other, totally soaked in sweat. They went to the mess room to cool off and wait to hear about the wall wash results."

"Don't keep me hanging."

"OK, so Mr. Tria comes out of the lab looking like his dog had just died. Ten ppm still, after all that work. So I told him to wait in my office, not to do anything, just to wait, and I'd be back in fifteen minutes. I went up to my cabin and got on my knees and invited God to intervene in this mess. I told him that I wanted everyone to know that He'd miraculously cleaned this tank. It was impossible, so only He could do it, and I would give him all the glory."

"So the tank's clean now?"

"Just let me finish the story, OK? So I go back downstairs after I pray, and I tell Mr. Tria to test it again. And he's like, 'But Chief, we haven't done anything. It's 10 ppm. Why should I test it again?' I told him, 'Just go back down the tank one more time, and run the test again. Trust me. Just do it.' So he does, but he's shaking his head because he thinks I'm crazy, and he's bone tired and doesn't want to see another ladder."

"So the tank's clean now?"

"I'm getting there — just let me tell you what happened, OK? So he comes back with the new sample, and he goes back in the lab, and a few minutes later he steps out again with his eyes as big as saucers and goes, 'What did you do, Chief?'

"'I didn't do anything.'"

"And he's like, 'But this is impossible. It's 10 ppm and then fifteen minutes later, without doing anything, it's 0 ppm? After working on it for days? It's impossible! What did you do? Where did you go?'"

"And I told him, 'I went to my cabin.'"

"Your cabin?"

"Yes, I went to my cabin."

"And he said like, 'Wha — but — what did you do in your cabin?'"

"'I prayed.' You should have seen his eyes then — they got even bigger! He went straight to the mess room, so within sixty seconds, every sailor on board knew that God had cleaned the tank for them."

"So what did they say?"

"Well, the consensus was that next time, I shouldn't wait so long to pray."

You can pray for anything, and if you have faith,
you will receive it."
- Matthew 21:22 NLT

THE SPEED OF LIGHT

There was no help for it - I was going to be late. Panic clenched my heart and my stomach flipped over. *Don't be ridiculous. It's not like you're facing a firing squad.* But panicked I was.

Today would be the third time I dropped my child off late for school. No big deal, right? Except that at his school, not only were the parents held responsible for students' tardiness, they were called into the Principal's office the third time the student was late, to be lectured like a child. I'd never been called into the Principal's office as a student, and I dang sure wasn't going to be called in as a parent!

Yes, actually, I was — once. And the fear of repeating that humiliation was causing me heart palpitations.

The first two times we were late were no doubt my fault. My son was only in the second grade, after all, and I had to drive him into town every morning. But today… It just wasn't right for me to be blamed for being late. I was doing everything in my power; and if we were late today, then that was just too blasted bad. I dug my mental heels in and psychically dared that principal to even look in my direction. But I knew my defiance wouldn't do any good. I'd be better off to humble myself and go willingly to my execution, taking responsibility for my…responsibilities.

But I WAS being responsible! That's what was galling me. My husband's flight was arriving at nine-thirty that morning, and there was no time to come home after dropping KJ at school. I had to head straight to the airport. Kevin had been overseas for a month and would arrive home exhausted to this cramped little travel trailer we were living in on site while we built our house. Being the neat freak that he was, he just couldn't really relax in a dirty house, so I wanted everything to be perfect and had spent the previous night cleaning and straightening. In such a tiny space, just one thing out of place made the whole trailer look messy. Add a 7-year old, a big dog and a couple of cats into the mix, not to mention the sea of red clay obligatory to Georgia construction sites, and it wasn't easy to keep our minuscule home looking tidy. Kevin worked so hard for us, and

I really wanted his surroundings to feel relaxing to him when he got home.

So I cleaned. And cleaned some more. And put the child to bed, and cleaned even more. It wasn't easy getting red clay out of light-colored carpet. Then I showered, washed my hair, shaved my legs — all the preparation for my husband's homecoming that could be done the night before. Knowing that we couldn't be late for school, I'd put out KJ's school clothes and my own clothes that night. Far from being a house mouse, all this preparation was proof I was excited about Kevin's arrival. It was also proof I was terrified of the Principal. Up half the night, still I set the alarm for an hour earlier than usual.

The kid was dressed and eating his breakfast, the beds were made and I was watching the clock as I put on my makeup. We absolutely had to leave home by 7:25 to make the last school bell at 8:00, and it was already 7:15. I still had to style my hair and finish dressing, and then there were the breakfast dishes to deal with. It just didn't seem fair — I'd stayed up so late, done everything I could possibly do ahead of time, gotten up early, and still there was more to do this morning than could possibly be done.

What should I sacrifice? Forget about looking my best at the airport? Abandon the idea of the house looking perfect? Or be late for school and face the Principal's humiliating lecture on how my child's tardiness disrupts the classroom?

"Hurry, Mom! You said we couldn't be late today."

Oh, Lord. Tell me what to do. What I'm trying to provide for my husband is surely scriptural. I know those two times we were tardy were my fault, but I'm truly doing my best today. I just CAN'T be called in by the Principal. The thought of it makes me break out in a cold sweat. Maybe to somebody else the house being perfect wouldn't be a big deal, but You know all this cleaning is an act of love. Please help me.

There was my answer -- turning it over to God. The realization hit me, and for perhaps the first time ever, I truly turned a problem over to Him. I knew what I wanted — for everything to be perfect for Kevin's homecoming and to not get in trouble for all the time it took to make it so. There was nothing I could do to make both of those things happen. But God could. So I told Him I was casting this care on Him.

Alright, Lord, I'm putting this in your hands. I don't see any possibility of getting my child to school on time if I do these meaningful things for my husband. So I'm trusting you to somehow keep me from getting in trouble with the school. I'm going to do everything that needs to be done here at home. I'm not going to waste any time, but I'm also not going to stress myself out, frantically trying to do the impossible. I'm just going to trust You to somehow make it all work out.

And that was that. I didn't give the time another thought. I did notice that after finishing my make-up and hair and washing, drying and putting away the breakfast dishes, we pulled out of the driveway at 7:40. That was ten minutes later than we'd EVER left home before. But I was completely at peace. (I later recognized this as the first time I'd ever fully and completely turned a problem over to God, because this was the first time I'd ever not even thought about the problem again.)

Traffic was heavy because it was later than usual, and I mentally scrolled through the landmarks and intersections we were going to pass — the Kroger grocery store at Hwy 20, then a long stretch of nothing before we passed a commercial area at the Honey Creek intersection, followed by another long stretch before traffic would really start piling up as we rolled into Conyers. Then we'd go through the stoplight at Hwy 138 and turn right when we got to Flat Shoals Road where the school was located. That part always took longer than expected due to congestion.

It seemed to take forever just to get to Kroger, but I wasn't anxious. I knew God was making a way for me. I chatted with my son, about what he was going to do in school that day as we drove on. He was excited that Dad would be picking him up. I looked up at the traffic light as we arrived at Honey Creek…

But we weren't at Honey Creek Road.

We were at Flat Shoals Road.

I shook my head, blinked a few times and looked around again. We were still at Flat Shoals. I would have rubbed my eyes, but didn't want to ruin my makeup. I signaled and turned right, and two blocks later turned right again into the school parking lot. I proceeded around the building where the line of cars was usually backed up. The line was so short it was scary. How late were we? Then lots of cars started filing in behind us. Was everyone running late this morning? I looked at the clock.

The line was short not because we were so late and everybody had already dropped off their kids, but because we were so early hardly anyone had arrived yet! It was 7:45. We'd left home ten minutes later than ever before, and arrived ten minutes earlier than ever before. The Lord of Heaven and Earth, the Creator of the universe, had bent time and space — overruled the laws of physics — just so I didn't have to go red-faced and terrified to the Principal's office.

Perhaps the bigger miracle, though, was that I was never late for drop-off again.

> ...do not be anxious about anything,
> but in everything by prayer
> and supplication with thanksgiving
> let your requests be made known
> to God. And the peace of God, which
> surpasses all understanding,
> will guard your hearts and your minds in Christ Jesus.
> – Philippians 4:6-7 ESV

DEJA VU ALL OVER AGAIN

You hear people talk about their life flashing before their eyes, but for me it was my child's life — his future, to be more precise. There was no doubt in my mind that my husband and I were about to die. But our six-year-old, strapped in the back seat? I saw how he would learn to lean on Jesus, how the Lord would comfort him. I had time, in my heart, for a conversation with the Holy Spirit about His tender care of my child, and I was at peace.

We had left home three hours later than planned, on the way to friends' home in central Georgia — about a four and a half hour drive. We often spent Saturday nights with them and attended Sunday morning service at their church. Then on Sunday nights, we visited the church we knew was to be our home church when we moved north. This particular weekend, our friend Sam was making his famous ribs, and our delay was quite an imposition. So we were tense, and Kevin and I were pushing each other's buttons. We'd been on the road about thirty minutes when he started looking for a teaching tape to listen to. I offered to help so he could keep his eyes on the country roads, but it earned me a rebuke. I decided I'd just be quiet and give him time to relax.

I turned to the back seat to check on my child and see what he needed — water, blanket, entertainment — when I felt the rumble strips in the road indicating we were approaching the dead end intersection where we turned toward a small town named Camilla. It was nearly dark now, our headlights were on, and I could see the reflective stop sign far ahead. I nearly mentioned the intersection ahead to Kevin, who was still fumbling with the stereo, but thought better of it — didn't want to tick him off further, and the rumble strips would alert him, anyway. I turned back to chat with our son.

As KJ and I talked, I suddenly realized we had not slowed down at all, and the rumble strip vibrations were very close together — like labor pains when time is up. I flipped around in my seat, and saw the sign — the STOP sign — only a few car lengths away. There was also another car approaching from the left. They had no stop sign from their direction. We were still doing seventy.

"KEVIN!"

He turned and looked at me. "What?" As if my screaming his name was as ordinary as asking him if he wanted a glass of sweet tea. I had no words of explanation — there was no time — and only stared at him, wide-eyed. I saw reality dawn on him just as I turned back to see the stop sign so close we should have been at a crawl, pulling to a stop. In my peripheral vision I saw him start spinning the wheel to turn left, while standing on the brakes, but my field of vision was quickly filling with the pine trees on the other side of the road as we passed the stop sign. That's when the vision of KJ's future began, and I found peace.

Beams of light, I assumed at the time from the oncoming car to our left, shone through our windows at crazy angles, and the pine trees seemed to shift as if our car was airborne and almost flipping, yet I felt no sense of lift or sway. Kevin was still spinning the steering wheel and hammering the brakes as I saw the stop sign approaching rapidly —

Wait…

We had already passed the stop sign.

Hadn't we?

Where was the oncoming car?

The road we were attempting to turn onto but had flown across… we were on it, the pine forest to our right. I felt the right rear tire slip off the pavement for half a second – the only indication we'd not made the turn perfectly. Then we were fully centered in our proper lane again as we continued slowing down to enter the city limits ahead.

Deep shaky breaths, trembling, and racing pulses occupied the front seat. In the back, KJ didn't seem to be aware anything had happened. I wondered what the people in the other car had seen. I wondered what I had seen.

Those were some good ribs.

Are not all the angels ministering
spirits sent out [by God]
to serve (accompany, protect) those who will
inherit salvation? [Of course they are!]
— Hebrews 1:14 AMP

FLYING FIRST CLASS

By the time we left the North Rim of the Grand Canyon, it was pitch black and we were exhausted. I didn't know then that I had sleep apnea, just that I never felt rested, and driving cross-country was problematic. The plan was to find a motel room and then drive the next day to Ogden, Utah to surprise my good friend with a visit. She was worse at staying in touch than I was; but I knew her address, and it was a school day so I knew she'd be home. Our sons, too, were long overdue for a visit, and despite excitement at the prospect of seeing his buddy the next day, my ten-year-old was dead to the world in the passenger seat.

There was no fuel available before getting on the road, but I wasn't worried. This was the single most famous landmark in the country. Fuel, food, and lodging couldn't be far away. The night had a thick heaviness to it, though, like tar. I'd never experienced a night sky so dark. Where were the stars? Behind the mountain and the trees, I figured.

Thinking of my friend, Libby, I wondered how she was really doing so far from her eastern hills of Virginia. She made me laugh, but she was tough — she'd been a drill sergeant in the Army. She loved me, and I never had the slightest qualm about leaving my son with her. She'd die before she let anything happen to him.

She'd taught me so much about living by faith, and I'd learned very quickly to do what she said and ask questions later. For instance, one particular day we were driving to the grocery store together when she said, "Take the next right." Knowing that was not the way to the grocery store, but to a residential area, I nonetheless turned. "Two or three blocks up, I think…that's it. That's the house. Just pull over." I didn't see anyone around, but I knew she was hearing something from above.

She was back in about ten minutes. When I gave her a questioning look, she said, "It was a little old white lady." (Libby was black, or everyone assumed she was. Primarily, she was Blackfoot.) "She looked up and saw me coming up in her backyard, and you know what she said? She said, 'You were sent to me'? I said, 'Yes, ma'am. What're you doing out here in this hundred-degree heat trying to mow your own lawn? I gotta get you back in the house. You gotta take better care of yourself.' So I set her down in her chair and got her some water and put the mower away."

I missed her terribly.

The road north began to climb steeply with a few twists and turns, but I'd driven the Rockies and other mountain ranges before, so it wasn't a problem. It just wasn't what I'd expected. *I've got this.*

There were no street lights, no light at all. No moon, no glow from oncoming headlights. I was alone on the road. The blackness seemed to absorb my headlights, and I was fighting to see. Why was my jaw hurting? Oh, I was clenching it. I took some deep breaths and tried to relax.

I jerked my head up. I'd just nodded off! Thank God I was on a straight stretch, but there were lots of curves ahead, and no shoulder to pull off on. *Lord, please help me.* I tried the radio, but there was only static, and I couldn't take my eyes off the road to deal with the CDs.

"Son, can you wake up? I need you to talk to me." He roused for about ten seconds then was fast asleep again. The switchbacks were closer and closer together now as we kept climbing. It wouldn't be so scary if the road wasn't so narrow. From what I could see, the ditch on my right side was just inches from the white line, and on my left, there was the single oncoming lane and then nothing — blackness that I had to assume was just air and a long fall. My head jerked up again. I panicked. Surely there must be somewhere to pull off this road! But if there was, I couldn't see it. I was having to steer by the headlights reflecting off the white line on my right just in front of the car. Why weren't my headlights illuminating anything? I couldn't just stop on a narrow two-lane road and wait for daylight. *Dear Lord, I need rescuing. Please don't let anything happen to my son.*

The next time I woke up, I couldn't see anything, including the road. It just wasn't there — nothing but black. There was no road noise. I tried the brakes, but our speed didn't change. I tried the accelerator, and the engine revved, but again, no change in speed. We were in mid-air. But I had no sensation of falling. I turned the steering wheel, having no idea what direction I should be turning, but it didn't seem to have any effect either. A moment later, I felt the road under the tires again, and I continued to try to navigate the switchbacks by the white line on the right. But I could not force my eyes to stay open for long. And even when they were open, I couldn't see enough to drive safely.

It happened again — that weightless sensation with no response from the steering, brakes or accelerator. Yet we were in motion. And again, the sensation of rubber meeting road returned. Three times this phenomenon occurred — I'd jerk myself awake to feel like I'd driven off the side of the mountain, only to be set on the right lane again.

A red glow ahead…stop sign! *Thank you, Lord.* We were on flat land again. I nearly cried. Choosing the direction to take, it was only about a mile before lights appeared ahead. I didn't even care they all said 'No Vacancy.' We'd been on 'empty' for a while when a convenience store with gas pumps finally appeared. Since no actual restaurants could be found open, we refueled both tank and tummies. By the time we came to a town large enough to offer more than fully booked mom and pop motels, and restaurants that closed at eight, I was bushy-tailed enough to keep driving.

We pulled into Libby's driveway about six a.m. She'd be so surprised! We'd be waking her a half hour early, but when she saw who was at her door…

That door opened before I reached the front porch. "Woman, what do you think you're doin' driving 'cross the country all by yourself, just this baby and you? I been up all NIGHT praying for you. You done lost your mind? Driving those mountains in the dark! God got me up in the middle of the night 'n made me get on my knees for you. You made good time, though. I'll say that. Get yourself in here, and get you some breakfast and some sleep. Boy, get in here. Go wake up your buddy, while I give your mama a piece of my mind."

> He stretches out the north over the void
> and hangs the earth on nothing.
> – Job 26:7 ESV

TEN FEET TALL AND BULLETPROOF

The phone is about to ring. It's okay, he's not hurt.

There was no reason to have been concerned — KJ wasn't even due home for an hour. The phone did ring, though. I answered it. My husband looked up and I mouthed to him, *"He's OK,"* before I even heard the caller's voice, which of course made my husband jump up and rush to my side.

We drove to the site. Conveniently, there was adjacent beach parking. My baby got a hug before a not-very-amiable cop put him in a squad car where he couldn't be coddled, and proceeded to apply a tongue-lashing that, to this day, I'm in the dark about.

I was reminded of a joke people who'd worked in the Arctic often tell about helicopters. KJ's jeep was unavailable for service. Was that because it was upside down, or because it was in the water?

Home was warm and light-filled and surprisingly peaceful. My husband told me a couple of days later what God had shown him as he'd sat on the side of the bed that night, thanking God for our son's safety. The Lord had reached out and held the Jeep back, just inches was all it took. Had He not, when the Jeep flew off the road, it would have been the driver's door, not the quarter panel, that landed on the boulder in the water, and KJ would have been pinned between the door and the steering wheel. My child's rib cage would have been crushed, puncturing his lungs and heart.

He may have thought at sixteen he was ten feet tall and bulletproof. But every day my child lives now is Grace.

— & —

The phone rang.

Yep.

There was no more Jeep, so he was riding the Vespa when he left the party. He knew to brake only, not swerve, for deer. But he also knew that if he hit the deer that had just jumped out in front of him with a Vespa, he was dead. So he swerved and went off the road into the towering firs that lined the shoulders of the street-light-free island we lived on. When Kevin and I arrived, a paramedic was holding my child's head immobile where he reclined in the passenger seat of a helpful passer-by's car.

Ambulance rides by ferry, all night in the ER for cervical and skull exams, we returned the next morning with only his arm in a sling. In daylight, his dad found the Vespa. He'd missed a fir tree by an inch — sixteen, ten feet tall, bulletproof.

—&—

Sixteen meant he was old enough to start aviation school, too. Yay! And since he'd only totaled two vehicles so far, why not buy him a Harley so he could road-trip with his dad, right?

Lord, he is yours. I relinquish all perceived control over his safety I ever thought to have. He was a gift from you, and I put him back into your hands. I trust you with my child.

Just before he completed his private license, at seventeen, I think, he was flying solo, landing at an airport he'd never flown into, in the dark. That was never supposed to happen. Unexpected snow flurries turned into a blizzard, the blizzard turned into — white out. God was with him. I heard he drank under-age beer later that night.

Who knows how many other close calls he's had that he hasn't told his mom about?

For the first wreck, God told me ahead of time that my child was unharmed, then showed his dad how He'd interrupted the vehicle's momentum — overriding the laws of physics — to save his life. He's not sixteen anymore, but with my God's merciful protection, he's still ten feet tall and bulletproof.

"Look!" Nebuchadnezzar shouted.
"I see four men, unbound, walking
around in the fire unharmed!
And the fourth looks like a god!"
– Daniel 3:25 NLT

FIFTY-SEVEN & THREE QUARTERS

"We'll move the kitchen archway to the far right, so when you enter the front door, my grandmother's gorgeous buffet will be straight ahead — much better than staring at the kitchen sink. Then we'll do what you said — open up into that first bedroom to make the dining area.

I'd put our huge home on the cliff on the market, subsequent to my husband's death, and was downsizing. Space planning was crucial.

"My grandmother's buffet doesn't store that much, but my Italian lacquer buffet does, so we'll need to leave this one section of the dining room wall to back it up against and build a small perpendicular wall to create a niche for it. The buffet is exactly sixty inches long, so just over five feet of usable space in the niche is crucial. I need the storage in the dining room, but also, I have nowhere else to put that buffet."

It was the first piece of serious furniture Kevin and I ever bought, so I would never part with it. Plus, it's like it's bigger on the inside than the outside, it stores so much — china, crystal, linens, serving pieces, you name it. I knew I'd be desperate for storage in this little house, especially with my mother downsizing at the same time and foisting china from earlier generations on me.

Months passed, and Terry, my renovator, finally got to the dining room. I reminded him a couple of times of the measurement required to house the Italian buffet. He calculated the drywall thickness on both sides of the niche, the size of the old studs he was re-using, the base moulding, even allowing for the coats of drywall mud and paint. He measured and re-measured, calculated and re-calculated, just to be safe, but it wasn't complicated. He built the wall, laid the floor, painted the walls and installed the trim.

With two households of furnishings going into a small home, and the mixture of my favorite antique family pieces and my own modern acquisitions, I had to learn to embrace glam eclectic maximalism — and love it. The two buffets epitomized the melding of styles — the ebony piece spoke of grandeur, the lacquered of sleek and shiny modernism. I was creating a unique decor, both sophisticated and fun. It was exciting. And it was good for me to have a project to sink my teeth into. It kept the trauma of the move without Kevin to a minimum.

The house was finally ready to receive my buffets. Until I measured — fifty-seven and three quarter inches. My stomach lurched. Three times I measured. I really thought I was going to be sick. It had to be at least sixty inches! I measured again. I needed that piece of furniture. It was important for sentimental reasons. Kevin and I had shopped for weeks. It was just as important for practical reasons. I was downsizing from thirty-eight hundred square feet to sixteen hundred. I needed the storage that buffet offered. I ran through the plan for every room of that house in my mind and could not find a spare inch of wall space to put that buffet against. I wailed for Terry to come.

He turned ashen when he measured and got the same length I had come up with. He had no explanation. He was completely baffled. There was no answer to be had. He had no idea how it had happened, and I had no solution. There was no way to change the placement of that wall now, not with the floor and trim installed, the ceiling smoothed. We just stood there, silent, staring at the wall — the fifty-seven and three quarter inch wall.

I tried to put it out of my mind. Every few weeks I'd measure again just to be sure. Fifty-seven and three quarter inches — frustration, ACUTE frustration flooded me every time. I'd designed that reno to accommodate every piece of furniture and art that was important to me. There was very little that I hadn't found a way to accommodate. Finally, the last time I measured, I whispered, "Lord, there's nothing I can do about this. I'm leaving it in your hands. I know you'll provide a solution of some kind. I'm not going to agonize over it any longer."

So I traveled over three thousand miles to rescue the other half of my furniture from ten years of storage and load up additional pieces that were being handed down to me. It was six months before I returned, and the twenty-seven-foot truck wouldn't have held another saucepan. The two buffets were among the most important of the cargo — one sleek and modern, the other a stately matte ebony with miniature Corinthian columns and hand-painted gold, even agate ornamentation. That new wall would create the visual barrier between the two, or at least that had been the plan.

The Italian lacquered buffet came off the truck in three pieces thanks to the movers ten years earlier, and one of the guys helping to unload asked, "Where to?"

Without thinking I answered, "Dining room. Just to the left of the front door. Terry's going to put it back together after the truck's been emptied."

Finally, everything was offloaded, and I wondered if I'd ever find anything again — between stuff stored in the attic, the shed, the house and more paid storage. As I entered my home, now crowded again with stacks of boxes, my eye fell first to my grandmother's gorgeous ebony buffet, already in the place of honor, destined to have a modern abstract painting above it. Then to my left, the three bubble-wrapped chunks of the modern Italian buffet demanded my attention. My beloved husband had actually invested time to select it with me. That had been such a fun time for me, to have his genuine, interested involvement in furnishing our first home. I wondered what I would do about the buffet now — maybe give it to our son? My heart wasn't ready to part with it. And where would I store the china?

Automatically, I extended the measuring tape I was holding, yet again.

Again I wailed Terry's name.

He came running to the dining room with a look of alarm. Perhaps he thought I'd hurt myself. I handed him the measuring tape. He gave me the same apologetic glance as the first time I'd called him in to measure the wall, many months earlier. "What do you want me to do?" he asked looking at the tape.

"Measure it."

He looked offended, like I was trying to rub his mistake in. But he measured the wall for the umpteenth time anyway, and came up with the same number I had just read.

Sixty and one half inches.
"Measure twice, pray once."

> For the eyes of the Lord are on the righteous
> and his ears are attentive to their prayer...
> – 1 Peter 3:12

− 3 −

PROTECTION

Guardian Angels - Your Own Secret Service

> "You can change the world again, instead of protecting yourself from it."
>
> - Julien Smith, <u>The Flinch</u>

> The enemy is not fighting you because you are weak, he's fighting you because you are strong.
>
> - Unknown

How many times does God protect us that we're unaware of? We're clueless of what may be ahead when that frustratingly slow driver from the prairies pulls out in front of us. How many NYC residents had unexpected delays on the way to work, September 11, 2001? Believe God for His protection, and walk fearless in His perfect love. (1 John 4:18)

Proof of God's Will

> Even though I walk through the valley of the shadow of death, I will fear no evil, for you are with me; your rod and your staff, they comfort me.
>
> - Psalm 23:4 ESV

My times are in your hand; rescue me from the hand of my enemies and from my persecutors!

- Psalm 31:15 ESV

Have I not commanded you? Be strong and courageous. Do not be frightened, and do not be dismayed, for the Lord your God is with you wherever you go.

- Joshua 1:9 ESV

God is our refuge and strength, a helper who is always found in times of trouble.

- Psalm 46:1 CSB

Now we will be saved from our enemies and from all who hate us.

- Luke 1:71 NLT

KETTLE FALLS

Since Kevin was from western Canada and I was from the Southeastern U.S., our trips to visit family were about as long as you go on a road trip. Our early-marriage trips we made on the Harley, both sets of parents chewing their fingernails down at either end of the trail.

We made a habit of going a different route each time we rode cross-country, seeing new places along the way. But we usually crossed into Canada from Washington State, which meant that by the time we got to Washington we were beginning to duplicate past routes. This would be our second ride over Sherman Pass. It's the highest mountain pass in Washington State that is maintained year-round. It was getting late the night we pulled into Kettle Falls, the town at one end of the pass, and we were running out of gas. And we were tired — so tired —and so, so cold.

The gas station we found was closed until morning. And that's when the trouble began.

I want you to understand that at that time in our lives neither Kevin nor I would have been recognized as Christians. Yes, we had been raised in Christian homes and baptized as kids, but I can't tell you it meant much to us at that time. But I would have been so grateful for a nudge of discernment from the Holy Spirit that night.

We stopped in at the police station, which was surprisingly busy, and asked if there was another gas station open and where we could get food and lodging. The answers were not what we'd hoped for. So we got directions to the bar that was apparently the only establishment other than the cop shop open.

A roaring fire was the main attraction, and I headed straight for the deep stone hearth with our helmets while Kevin paid for food and drinks. Pepperoni sticks and chips for dinner — great. A table surrounded by locals was near us. They looked like they could be loggers, or wannabe bikers — maybe just guys the folks we had just spoken with at the cop shop would be familiar with. Who knew? But they were friendly enough.

"You just passing through?"

"Yeah, it's been a long day on the road."

"Where you from?" The conversation progressed, and they invited us to join them at their table. After a while, one guy went outside for a moment. In hindsight, I think he was checking out our motorcycle, but at the time, we were just enjoying their company and the warmth of the fire.

After hanging out for an hour or so, the top dog said, "There's no place to stay around here. Where 'ya gonna stay tonight? It's dang cold."

"Yeah, it is. We thought there'd be a motel open."

"Well, I guess you can sleep on the floor at our place. We rent a house on the mountain."

"Thanks, but I'm outta gas," Kevin said. "We'll just have to find a windbreak to huddle up behind until the gas station opens at six."

"We're not that far up the mountain, and I can see your wife's still frozen. Tell you what. Follow us, and if you run out of gas, we'll stop and siphon a little out of the truck. That way you can at least lay down and be warm for the night. It's no problem — you'd be welcome."

Warmth. I looked at Kevin, and he knew I'd give most anything to not have to be outside for the next four or five hours. You also need to understand that putting up strangers passing through was a common hospitable trait in the biker community, so this offer wasn't a big surprise or anything new to us. We'd certainly had strangers in our home before and become good friends.

"OK, we really appreciate the offer. But keep a close eye on me behind you because I really don't think I can get far on what's in the tank — especially going uphill."

We all headed out a few minutes later. As three guys jumped in the back of the truck and the other two opened the cab doors, one called to me, "You should come ride in the truck with us where it's warm." Wonderful idea. I headed in that direction.

"That's OK. She'll ride with me." What? There was a heater in the truck. I stood on the sidewalk staring at my husband like he was torturing me.

"Get. On. The bike." He said in low tones I'd never heard before. I got on the bike.

We followed the truck out of the small town and up a steep, paved two-lane lined with driveways. Up we went, curving around and around the mountain. Kevin became very concerned about gas, but the bike kept going. And going. And going…and going…and going. We'd driven miles, and with every mile, the knot in my stomach got tighter. I was finally understanding what Kevin's street smarts had told him from the beginning. He knew what those men were planning as soon as we ran out of gas. "I don't know how we've made it this far, but those guys were lying through their teeth. We've gone over ten miles. We're turning around."

"Can we make it back to town?"

"We'll coast most of the way down the mountain and hopefully have enough gas to get to the police station." He followed the truck's tail lights until they went around a sharp bend ahead, buying us time to turn around without them realizing it. Now my shivering was from fear. I knew they could catch us if they figured out we'd headed back and we ran out of gas before we got to the police. They'd take the Harley. And they'd take me. That meant they'd have to kill my husband.

Kevin maneuvered the mountain turns using as little engine power as possible while going as fast as possible. He had skills. Somehow, we made it across town to the welcoming lights of the cop shop. I doubt there's ever been a biker that happy to enter a police station. We told an officer what had happened, which was nothing, so there was no official report — only knowing nods, raised eyebrows and an invitation to sit up in their brightly lit waiting area all night. We were grateful.

At 6 a.m. on the dot, we rolled into the gas station. Under their awning there was finally enough light to see into the gas tank. It was bone dry.

> Rescue me from evil people, O LORD.
> Keep me safe from violent people.
> They plan evil things in their hearts...They have set traps for me along the road. [Selah]... O LORD Almighty, the strong one who saves me, you have covered my head in the day of battle.
> – Psalm 140:1-7 GWT

JESUS, TAKE THE WHEEL

Being from South Georgia, driving in snow and ice isn't my forte. Now I live in Canada. It's the garden belt of Canada, but we do get snow occasionally.

One winter night on the way home, I hit ice. I found myself completely unable to control what my car was doing. Braking made me go faster. Steering was suddenly impossible. Counter-steering didn't work either. I began to spin down the two-lane road. Not knowing if anyone was heading toward me, I was using both lanes as I pirouetted from the oncoming lane's shoulder to my own and back again. It would have been awesome had I been on ice skates, competing for the Olympic team, but in my van, speeding up and out of control, it was terrifying.

I let go of the steering wheel and shouted, "JESUS!"

That was all it took. My vehicle that had been accelerating against my will, spinning and careening from lane to lane was slowing down. It stopped spinning and moved into the correct lane without me steering. Then it came to a gentle stop on the shoulder without me braking.

The van sat idling, which was amazing itself, because I normally have to keep my foot on the brake if I want to sit still. I put it in park and turned on the emergency blinkers while I took a few minutes to stop shaking. When my breathing was steady, I pulled back onto the road, turned left, and went home to tell my husband that the Lord had done it again.

> For it is written: He will give his angels orders concerning you, to protect you,
> – Luke 4:10 CSB

WALKING IN JESUS' IMMUNITY

Really nasty flus and viruses tend to go around our little island every year, and I was so sick I wanted to die. In fact, the illness had led me into a deep depression that I can't really explain, but I truly wanted to die. Then I heard the spirit of death speak so clearly it was as if it was in the bed next to me. I turned my head and laughed in its face, and it took off like a scalded cat. I knew that if he was telling me to die, that I would be recovering by morning and all would be well. I was right — it's always darkest before the dawn.

The day my husband died, I remembered that experience two winters earlier. *Lord, you're going to have to keep me well, because at this point, if I catch something that bad again, I might as well go ahead and plan my own funeral while I'm planning Kevin's. I will not be able to stand against it when deep-down I'd rather be in heaven.*

Stress inhibits the human immune system, and I was entering the most stressful year of my life. Nonetheless, I did not catch a single communicable disease — no colds, no flu, no anything. I made a point of hugging people who didn't feel well, because, well, who doesn't need a hug when they're not well? Sometimes they'd back away, not wanting to infect me, but I'd hug them anyway.

In fact, at the time of this writing, it's been nearly six years since my husband's death, and I have never been sick — except for once…

— & —

I was having a conversation with myself (no, not out loud) about what I would say the next time I had an opportunity to share with somebody about walking in Jesus' immunity.

No, seriously, I really haven't caught a single cold or flu in two-and-a-half years!

Then I heard, "Wow — two-and-a-half years? That's a long time. Isn't it about time He let you do it yourself?"

(Laughing) Yeah, really…

What? What had I just said? That wasn't me saying I should do it myself! *No! I take it back! That's not what I meant!*

By morning I felt it coming. No standing on Jesus' authority, binding, or rebuking seemed to make any difference, and I can't really explain that. By night, I was sick as a dog.

Weeks later, I said to my mom, "How could that one errant thought do so much damage?"

"That's all it took for Peter to start sinking."

Right.

It took a couple of months for me to feel confident again in His covering me — not about His covering, but of my living in it. Since then, I've never doubted it, and I've never been sick.

—&—

That's not to say the enemy hasn't TRIED to make me ill. I'm going to go down a rabbit hole here and share something that isn't a miracle story. It's too a good an opportunity to pass up, to make a couple of important points.

Once in 2019, that feeling hit me suddenly. I was sharing my first book with somebody — the one about healing (*Disarming Deadly Doctrines -- Stop Sickness in its Tracks with Head-Smacking Revelations of God's Will*). You know that feeling — hot and clammy alternately, fuzzy-headed, achy, exhausted, just wanting to lie down. I tried to fight it off while I was still visiting with my friend, but I needed to be able to get aggressive. I finally headed to bed about midnight. I could sense malevolence. This was a spiritual attack, which is not the same as your immunity blocking contagions. Nobody in the house had been ill and nobody became ill later. This was a demonic attack, and I knew it was trying to kill me. I could feel its hatred.

I fought that thing — speaking the Word, binding and loosing, standing in dominion and casting it away. It was so difficult because I was already exhausted and feverish. But I won. It gave up about 4:00 a.m. Resist the devil, and he will flee from YOU.

So, my points here are:

1. The enemy comes only to kill, steal and destroy. The Bible tells us this but we take it too lightly. Your sniffles aren't just a common cold. Our adversary is hoping to turn it into double pneumonia and kill you.
2. You can walk in Jesus' immunity, but there can also be occasional physical assaults that you must repel because Jesus already gave you the tools to do so — namely His authority to use. I do not mean that the Lord won't help you, but God left kings in the Promised Land for the Israelites to practice warfare on. He wants you to learn spiritual warfare because that's your job, and you need to get good at it. So when the devil attacks suddenly, know how to fight him off.
3. Our words have great power.

They are free from common human burdens;
they are not plagued by human ills.
– Psalm 73:5 NIV

JESUS, THE REAL FIRST RESPONDER

A very similar thing happened to my husband once. We were having a dinner party. The guests of honor, my brother and sister-in-law, had come 3,200 miles. It was the last night of their visit and we had several other guests present. We were about five minutes away from sitting down to the table when I sent Kevin on a quick errand to get extra chairs. A few minutes later, I started putting food on the table and was wondering what was taking him so long. Eventually, I had everyone take their places and begin eating. Then I excused myself. I found my husband in bed, shivering violently with cold and pain, burning with fever, eyes shut, barely able to speak. What could have happened? When I sent him downstairs, he was smiling, energetic and perfectly well.

I appointed a friend to play host and returned to Kevin. For some reason I felt I needed to get him up. I supported him in his weak state to the family room where I situated him in his recliner. Several times I had to get him up and into the bathroom, into the shower, dry and warm again and back into his chair.

I couldn't find a thermometer even though I knew I had several, so I phoned a nearby friend with children, knowing she'd have one handy. We'll call her Allie. I told her I'd send someone over to pick it up, but she said, "No. I'm on my way."

When she arrived minutes later, she urged me to phone 911. I was disappointed. I had hoped she'd just pray with me and all would be well. But she was alarmed at Kevin's condition. He couldn't speak, and he didn't even have the energy to nod in agreement. His jaws were clenched, every muscle was tense, and he was blistering hot. So I phoned the paramedics, hoping they'd at least be able to explain what was happening to my husband. Being on an island, the only other emergency medical help was a ferry ride away.

Once the 911 call was made, Allie appeared to just think for a moment, then said, "Something is here. Do you mind if I pray over Kevin?" She had much more experience in spiritual things than I had at that time, so I was thinking, *Don't waste time asking me if it's OK -- just do whatever needs doing!*

She prayed and asked for some water to anoint Kevin. "Don't you mean oil?"

"No, I need water this time." I got the water, then understood why the Lord had not sent me for oil. She said, "It's not in Kevin, or exactly on him, it's in the room." She sprinkled water into the air with her fingers all around the room as she prayed and cast the spirit out of the house. I thanked God also for not sprinkling oil all over my living room.

The paramedics were at the door. One was a friend — we'll call her Dana. As captain of the ferry when home from his regular job overseas, Kevin worked closely with emergency personnel on our island, and he had a lot of respect for Dana. They took Kevin's vitals, making note of his high temp, racing pulse and skyrocketing blood pressure. He didn't answer when they asked questions. His eyes were still shut tight. We waited and observed, and I answered what questions I could. Allie prayed in tongues under her breath from a distance. Time dragged.

Dana kept checking her watch. She took Kevin's pulse several times, and reminded me that I'd soon have to decide whether or not to take Kevin to the hospital because the last ferry of the night was leaving in 45 minutes.

"No hospital." We all jumped when Kevin spoke. His eyes were still closed, but his jaw had relaxed some. So had his fists. The shivering wasn't so bad. He didn't say anything else. Dana checked his vitals again and found them somewhat improved.

"We have about a ten-minute window until we have to decide whether or not to load him in the ambulance."

"I'm not going anywhere." Kevin took a deep breath, opened his eyes and said, "I'm fine." They checked his vitals again, which were now nearly normal. Dana was double-checking all the numbers, wondering what was going on. A minute later, Kevin repeated himself, "I'm OK now. You don't have to stay."

But Dana wasn't going anywhere yet. This was too strange. She wasn't trusting that whatever this was, was over. She checked vitals again.

Kevin was flexing joints, loosening up muscles that had been clenched in pain. In a span of about fifteen minutes, he went from extremely and inexplicably ill to smiling, laughing, and apologizing to the paramedics for causing them to be called out. The minutes had seemed like hours while staring at Kevin, waiting to see what would happen next. But the entire episode, from the time Allie had cast the demon out of our home, had only been about thirty minutes.

Casting out demons is not a miracle. It's something WE do ourselves using Jesus' authority. It's a matter of proclamation, as opposed to prayer. It's warfare. But it does result in our protection, and it certainly is a result of God's power, not our own. Just try casting out a demon in your own strength, and see what happens.

By the way, people who have strong men with them for protection when doing deliverance and caution others to do likewise, are not fully walking in Jesus' authority or in faith. The Word says you SHALL do these things and you SHALL in no way be harmed. I could tell you stories… and someday I will.

When evening came, they brought to Him many who were under the power of demons, and He drove out the spirits with a word and restored to health all who were sick.
– Matthew 8:16 AMPC

THE AXLE OF POWER

Just under four hours will get you from my new home to Lake City, FL — that is, if your vehicle is in working order. An uneventful trip is a good trip. Pulling out of my driveway, I said, "What is that vibration?" Not an indicator of an uneventful trip ahead.

I was speaking to my younger friend and helper, Marie, who could "mechanic" with the best of them if she has the right equipment and sometimes an assistant that can apply some brute force to the job at hand. We stopped to fill up, and she checked the tires and what she could see under my car, but all appeared fine.

Also along for the ride was a woman I'd never met until that morning, but who was in dire need of healing. And it just happened that we were headed to a conference where healing would be available in abundance. So off we went.

But by the time we arrived in Lake City, I was concerned about the worsening vibration I felt in the steering wheel.

It goes without saying that the conference was wonderful. The leader, Curry Blake, met with my new friend in person during the morning break, and she was healed. At lunchtime, Marie and I went looking for a tire shop. We were told I had a bent rim, that they could sell me a new one for $135, or I could wait and replace it when I got home. Marie said she knew people and could get me one for free. Since it didn't present a safety problem, according to the rim guy, I opted to wait and avail myself of Marie's network of car people.

On Saturday, the vibration took a turn for the worse, but it was impossible to find help on the dinner break. Walmart's tire center was open, but it turned out they did nothing but change out tires for ones they sold, and had no rims in stock.

That evening, back at the church, the healing service was taking place and we were instructed to write our prayer requests on cards and turn them in. The staff was to pray over them.

"Marie, put the car down as a prayer request. I'm going to, too." Driving back to the hotel that night was downright scary.

The next morning, however, driving back for the Sunday Service at the host church, the vibration seemed a little less violent. And it seemed to improve somewhat while we were in church. We decided not to look for a mechanic before driving home. As we pulled onto the interstate after getting fuel, the drive smoothed right out, and I hardly noticed any vibration at all on the four hour, uneventful trip.

However, a couple of days later, when Marie and her strong friend got under my car to do the needed work, we fully realized the fruit of that prayer request. That axle, which should have been straight, was bent like a dog's leg. There was no way, in the natural, that it would even have stretched across the distance of my car's width, it was so damaged. The evidence made it obvious that angels fueled by faith had gotten us home safely. 'THAT'S the God I serve.'

> But he said, 'What is impossible with man is possible with God.'
> – Luke 18:27

– 4 –

HEALINGS
It's All About Freedom

> A man's health can be judged by which he takes two at a time - pills or stairs.
> — Joan Welsh

> The foundation of success in life is good health: that is the sub-stratum fortune; it is also the basis of happiness. A person cannot accumulate a fortune very well when he is sick.
> — P. T. Barnum

Healing, according to many, is not technically a miracle, but simply a speeding up of the natural self-healing process God created our bodies to perform. Skin cells forming to heal a cut is a basic example. Healing that occurs due to replacement of missing organs, lengthening of limbs, growing new nerves or muscles, removal of metal from the body — those sorts of "healings" are definitely miracles, whether creative or by the superseding of natural laws. And many healings, both in Jesus' earthly ministry and now, are actually deliverances. The boy with what sounds like epilepsy and the stooped woman in the synagogue come to mind first. "Woman, thou art loosed…" (Luke 13:12)

Some people classify raising the dead separately from healing. Yes, that happens today, so much more than you know. I personally know four people who were raised. One was dead for several hours after her car was hit by multiple vehicles, one for three days (died of a fever as a child — see *Disarming Deadly Doctrines*). The other drowned, his body was recovered, and his eyes had turned white before the paramedics arrived. The fourth one you'll read about here.

I'm grouping all these types together under the umbrella of Healings for simplicity, as they all apply to our physical bodies. As you read these testimonies, take note of whether it was a healing, a creative miracle, deliverance, a raising, or a combination.

Going forward, keep in mind that living in divine health is God's best for us.

Proof of God's Will

> If the Spirit of God, who raised Jesus from death, lives in you, then he who raised Christ from death will also give life to your mortal bodies by the presence of his Spirit in you.
>
> - Romans 8:11 GNT

> And wherever He went—villages and towns and countrysides—they laid the sick in the marketplaces and begged Him just to let them touch the fringe of His cloak. And all who touched Him were healed.
>
> - Mark 6: 56 BSB

> *You know of* Jesus of Nazareth, how God anointed Him with the Holy Spirit and with power, and *how* He went about doing good and healing all who were oppressed by the devil, for God was with Him.
>
> - Acts 10:38 NASB

> …"Why are you looking among the dead for the living one? He's not here. He has been brought back to life!…
>
> - Luke 24:2-7 GWT

always bearing about in the body the dying of Jesus, that the life also of Jesus may be manifested in our body.

- 2 Corinthians 4:10 ERV

RAISING A CHILD

"You're pregnant, yes, but you're not going to have a baby."

That was obvious from the ultrasound screen. The embryo was caved in, shriveled up, nothing the way it was supposed to look. And I'd been cramping horribly for two weeks. Sailing with my husband for months, this was the first time since suspecting I was pregnant that I'd had shore access. My eyes were glued to the screen as the doctor continued her ultrasound examination. She surprised me by going 360 degrees around me — very thorough, or perhaps looking for some reason for the miscarriages. She found nothing suspicious other than what would have been my child. This was my fourth rodeo.

"If you don't expel it soon, come back and we'll do a DNC."

Iced tea and a view of the water may have been calming, but it wasn't comforting. The hotel's terrace was quiet that time of day, and I was hoping that the older American woman I'd befriended would show up soon. I really needed to talk. We'd spent a lot of time together, compatriots in a foreign land, and shared deep thoughts more readily than new friends would under normal circumstances. I could pour my heart out to her, and she'd mother me.

Instead, one of the cameramen I'd met there wandered up when he saw me. I guess it was obvious I wasn't my usual friendly self because his expression turned serious as soon as we made eye contact. I'd met a lot of media types since checking in, because all the presidential candidates and their entourages were in the same hotel, including Imelda Marcos.

Having sailed for years with Filipino crew, I knew they had a completely different view of what subjects were off-limits in conversation. I remembered one night on the ship, during a leaving-port party, one guy had asked me a series of increasingly pointed questions until I was beginning to squirm in my seat and look for a way out. Then he said, "Could I ask you a personal question?" I know I must have blanched. "Do you like pizza?"

So when this kind man started asking me what was wrong, I told him. He grabbed my hands, dropped his head and began praying. I had no idea what he was saying because he'd reverted to his native Tagalog, but I knew his intent. I hadn't been in church for fourteen years, and had I leaned only on what I had learned growing up in a denominational church, I would have brushed the prayer off as a sweet gesture. But when I had first moved to Canada with my husband, I was drawn by the news coverage to a show called the 700 Club. I'd become fascinated at what they called *words of knowledge* and the phone calls reporting healings that came in every night. There I had learned about receiving what was prayed over you.

So when he prayed for me, I received that healing. Peace flooded me with the knowledge that one day, I would have a healthy baby.

I relaxed into my temporary life of luxury as an expatriate as time passed. Then one morning I suddenly realized I hadn't miscarried yet, and I went back to the clinic to find out if I needed to have a DNC. In that case, I would head home immediately. The doctor greeted me, checked the dates, and raised her eyebrows upon realizing it had been five weeks since my examination. She prepared the ultrasound for round two.

And there he was, in the middle of a workout apparently, just as busy and active as could be.

"How is this possible?" I exclaimed. You said I wasn't going to have a baby. It was dead, shriveled and dried up. I saw it with my own eyes!"

The doctor shrugged, and with a smile said, "It's a good thing we didn't do a DNC, isn't it?"

"But, I saw it." My head was swimming. I kept throwing out ideas, searching for some explanation. "Was it twins, maybe? And one died? Was there another one we didn't see?"

"No, we went all the way around you, remember? We were very thorough. There was no second baby. This is the only baby."

"But that baby was dead."

Apparently, Filipinos are not so surprised by the dead coming back to life.

Stretching out on the unfamiliar bed a week later in a Manila hotel, starting my journey home, I felt the first flutter of life. Our son was born perfect in every way, on the exact day I knew was his due date, defying the doctors and proving his mom right — such a good boy. Yet it was years before I realized that God had not only brought him back to life, He'd sped up our baby's development. God had redeemed the time — every single day of it — that our baby had been dead.

> And when the Lord saw her, he had compassion
> on her and said to her, "Do not weep."...
> And he said, "Young man, I say to you, arise."
> And the dead man sat up and began to speak,
> and Jesus gave him to his mother.
> – Luke 7:13-15 ESV

STRIKE TWO

WHAM! It hit me like a ton of bricks. Sweat broke out on my forehead and I ran for the bathroom. My child was sick, but I'd been sure I wouldn't catch it. And now I was reeling — high fever, dizziness, vomiting… the list of symptoms was long. But worse was the shame of realizing just how sick my son was and not once had I prayed over him. Well, now I knew, and I was getting angry. I turned that anger at myself to the original source of the problem — the enemy.

"I WILL NOT TOLERATE THIS SICKNESS! Not in my son, not in myself, so get out! In the Name of Jesus be gone! I bind the foul spirits of infirmity right now in the mighty Name of Jesus. You cannot remain in this household. We belong to Jehovah God and are redeemed by the Lamb! Get out!"

I literally stomped my feet for emphasis — not certain whether it was to show the enemy I meant business or for building my own bravado — I was new to this. I was sincere, though, and I was so angry at what was making my child feel the way I now understood he felt. I wasn't letting that go on another minute.

I kept that up for what felt like a long time, but was probably only about five minutes. I'd never attacked the darkness that way before, and I think it was so shocked it didn't know what to do. Resist the devil, and he will flee from you — that's what the Bible says, and it's true. That sickness took off like a scalded cat. It had been strike two, then I hit it over the fence.

I felt that thing leave me. Crossing the room, I sat on the bed beside my little boy and stroked his sticky back. In a moment he rolled over toward me and blinked his eyes, soft hair matted against his damp skin. "Mom. You sure are noisy. Can we watch a movie?"

This was the first time I experienced the power of using my authority in an emergency. If you are saved, you have that same authority. Have you ever put it to use? You can roar like the Lion of Judah — you are powerful with the Holy Spirit in you. When you first use this power, you'll realize how it is that Jesus could say that we who believe SHALL lay hands on the sick, cast out demons, and raise the dead. It's Him doing the work, all we have to do is be obedient. Rise up, church! You've got the power.

> "Truly I tell you, the one who believes in me will also do the works that I do..."
> – John 14:12 NASB

WALKING THE LINE

Months before my husband and I met, he was in a horrible motorcycle accident that claimed the life of the friend he was riding with. If the car had hit them ten seconds earlier, it would have been Kevin who died instead of his buddy.

As it was, Kevin flew so high into the air, that when he landed 110 feet down the road, he came straight down, no road rash from sliding, landing on his head and his left foot. He must have been bent like a bobby pin. He was wearing a helmet, of course, and it was in many pieces, but from a fall of such an incredible height, God's hand had to have caught him. There was no broken neck, no brain damage. He didn't even have a goose egg.

What he did have, though, was a shattered leg. His lower left leg was turned completely around. The paramedics had to cut his boot off to figure out which way to turn the leg so that they didn't twist it the rest of the way off before they strapped him onto a gurney.

He doesn't remember any of this. He remembers waking briefly in the LifeFlight helicopter, then again in emergency, then a couple of days later in horrible pain. Both bones were shattered, like the shell of a hardboiled egg after you've tapped it lots on the counter so you can peel it easily. In the first surgery, they laid down a type of netting to hold the tiny fragments in place, and placed them painstakingly around a vitalium rod. Plates and long screws were added, with layers of stitches and staples. Later came a full leg cast, which he was wearing when I met him. At our wedding, he wore a leg brace under his slacks and used a beautiful cane, a gift from his Best Man, at our wedding.

Miracle #1: He survived, and was without brain injury.

Miracle #2: They put his leg back together against all odds.

> ...Your wound is incurable and
> your injury is serious...
> For I will restore you to health And I
> will heal you of your wounds...
> – Jeremiah 30:12,17 ESV

— & —

Kevin was scheduled for a skin graft three days after we were married so that he could return to work on his ship. We had been telling the doctor for two months that his leg was infected but the doctor wouldn't listen. When Kevin came out of surgery, the plastic surgeon, who we'd never met before (we'll call him Dr. Jones), told us he wasn't able to complete the operation — there was nothing to graft to. By the time he'd debrided the wound (removed all the dead and infected tissue), there was a large hole in Kevin's leg clear down to the bone. He diagnosed Kevin as having osteomyelitis, a bone infection, and there was already a red line going up his calf that nobody had been able to see because it was covered by the cast. So the IVs started.

Kevin was on Vancomycin IV. That was in 1981, and Vancomycin is still the strongest antibiotic known to man. There was no effect the first few days, so the plastic surgeon visited us and told us that we had to watch that red line. If it continued up Kevin's leg, there was no way to save his life except to take the leg. Once the red line got into his thigh and close to his trunk, the infection would go systemic and kill him. We'd been married one week.

The doctor came every day. He'd taken over our case from the horrible doctor that had ignored us for two months and may have cost Kevin his leg, if not his life. Every day we watched that red line get a little longer. Every day Dr. Jones and his nurse pulled up the pig-skin covering the hole in Kevin's shin, and used a sterile instrument to reach down into the wound and tap. And every day he tapped on vitalium and bone. No change.

The nurses were great. I stayed full time, sleeping in a chair or on a couch in a waiting room if I could find an empty one. Showers didn't work for Kevin since he had to keep his leg dry, so I'd take him down the hall to a bathing room. We'd be there a long time. It had one of the only locking doors in the whole hospital, I think. One of the nurses brought us a rubber ducky, joking that we needed something to play with since we were in the bathing room for such extended periods.

Tiny absorbent pellets were poured into the wound every day, and they would soak up any infection (pus). Then distilled water was used to wash the pellets out, and new pellets were poured in. Soon, since I was there 24/7, I was changing Kevin's bandages and irrigating the wound every six hours instead of the nurses. I was the gatekeeper. If Admitting tried to put anybody that had any kind of infection into the second bed, I raised Cain. If I didn't think the pain medication was adequate, I raised Cain. If Kevin didn't get the food he ordered, you got it, I raised Cain. All in all, the nurses liked me — but I was going to make sure my new husband was well taken care of.

Every two days the phlebotomist came to change the IV. She wasn't that great at hitting veins. And Vancomycin is very hard on veins anyway. So Kevin had knots in his arms and burned out veins and bruises everywhere. It was painful. So why, we asked, when she hit a good vein at the proper angle and the drug wasn't burning it, couldn't we leave the IV alone for a few more days or until it started giving him problems? It only made sense. Apparently, hospital policy trumped common sense. So every two days, she poked him and stuck him and bled him and bruised him. One day he'd had enough. He took off his tee shirt to show off his tattoos, pumped up his muscles, and when she came in, he gave her his hardest bad boy biker glare and said, "Lady, you've got one shot, and one shot only. You'd better hit that vein or I'm coming out of this bed." Her hands were shaking like a leaf. But she hit the vein. Amazing what a little motivation will do.

But through all this we were terrified. If he lost his leg, how would we live? How could he go back to work? Hourly we watched powerless as slowly but steadily The Red Line inched upward.

So many people were praying for us. The hospital chaplain visited a few times and really made a difference — or at least began the process of making a difference. If he'd come more often, I'm sure we would have rededicated our lives during our hospital stay. I even prayed for him to come more often. But as the weeks passed, he seemed to have gone on vacation.

Dr. Jones, as it turned out, was a Christian. But now he only came every other day, because there were no changes to observe. He knew we were watching The Red Line. The nurses were watching The Red Line. There was no need for him to watch it, too. So every other day he came, and every other day we heard *tap, tap, tap* on the bone.

After a month, Kevin had endured just about all the hospital life he could handle. He was crabby, always in pain on some level even if it was just soreness from laying in bed all day and being a pincushion. He was afraid for his life and his leg, and he complained constantly. The lack of privacy was really getting to me. And it was hard, being scared myself, to always be supportive and cajoling with Kevin. I was gaining weight, too, as the highlights of our days were General Hospital on TV, which we'd become totally addicted to for lack of anything else to do, and midnight cheeseburgers from the coffee shop downstairs. My trousseau wasn't fitting so well.

About five weeks in, I remember so clearly Kevin saying, "If I could just go home, I would be the perfect patient. I'd be so happy if I could just sit in the recliner and look out the window. I wouldn't even complain about not being able to ride when a Harley went by. I just want to hear those engines again."

Six weeks after checking into the hospital, as I was changing Kevin's bandage, something was different. I was intimately acquainted with that wound, and I knew something was different. But it was so subtle that I couldn't put my finger on what it was. Kevin noticed that I had stopped moving and was staring at his leg.

"What is it? What's wrong?" He couldn't see it, of course, because he was in traction.

"Nothing's wrong. I'm just looking at it." I applied the fresh bandaging, but was on pins and needles for the next six hours because I knew something was happening under that gauze.

Time to change the bandages again, and I tried my best to appear nonchalant. When I pulled back the last layer, it was a shock. "I'll be right back."

"Where are you going? What's going on?" Kevin was understandably alarmed.

"It's ok, really. I just want a nurse to see this and make sure it's not my imagination."

I grabbed one of our favorite nurses in the hallway. "Please, come quick. You need to look at Kevin's wound. I think it might be better."

Elizabeth's eyebrows jumped toward her hairline, and she dropped what she'd been doing to quickstep it into our room and see for herself. She looked at Kevin's leg, ignoring his queries as I had. She looked at me. She looked back at the leg. She looked at me again. "I think you may be right."

"WHAT?! What is it?"

"Baby, I think your leg is getting better."

Six hours later, there was no doubt.

From that point on, it was a thrill to change those bandages. That hole was closing so rapidly it was like watching a time-lapse film of a flower unfolding, but in reverse. And The Red Line was fading and receding just as rapidly. It was miraculous. There was no other word for it, and there was no doubt Who was making it happen. But Dr. Jones was unable to attend us that night due to emergency surgery, so by the time he arrived the following evening, the difference from three nights earlier was shocking. Still, he took his tools and probed the wound to see how deep he could get. I don't really understand why that never hurt Kevin, but he didn't seem to mind it. The doc prodded and probed, then looked up at us and asked, "Why are y'all still here? Why haven't you gone home yet?"

I tucked my face into Kevin's shoulder and cried.

The doctor was back the next morning to remove the staples, which Kevin said didn't hurt, but I turned green and nearly passed out. I sat down, knowing that if I passed out they'd have to take me to the ER and it would only prolong our stay. Before leaving, this wonderful doctor made sure we understood what had happened. "I had nothing to do with the healing, you know — it's all God." But we already knew that.

We were soon home. Kevin on crutches made his way to the recliner, which I'd turned to face the sunny window, and he smiled as he relaxed into its comfort. I took him some juice and put a couple of pillows under the leg to keep it high. It was the first time he'd looked content since the end of our 3-day honeymoon.

A Harley rode by. "How much longer am I going to have to sit here in this blasted chair while the whole world goes by without me?"

Miracle #3: He survived osteomyelitis, without amputation. God got all the glory.

Miracle #4: Financial — We probably would have owed him about $50,000.00, but our bill from our favorite plastic surgeon was only $500. I mentioned this to my grandmother, and she smiled… seems she'd gotten to know Dr. Jones one day when she was visiting us, and it turned out that he was a member of the church she and my grandfather had donated the land for. Thank you , Dr. Jones — you know who you are.

> Asa became diseased in his feet, and his malady became increasingly severe. Yet even in his illness he did not seek the LORD, but only the physicians. So…Asa died and rested with his fathers.
> – 2 Chronicles 16:12,13 BSB

— & —

1992, eleven years later, Kevin was having back problems, and we discovered it was due to his left leg being shorter than his right. The lower leg was misshapen and the foot turned outward, but it never gave him a minute of trouble other than the back issue. So after a very successful surgery to repair a herniated disc, we started having Kevin's left shoes raised by resoling and by adding a small heel insert. No big deal.

Except that Kevin needed runners for work, and as the years went by it became more and more difficult to find runners that were made with soles that could be removed and built up. Add to that, the runners didn't last long due to the deteriorating effects of oil and chemicals on the decks of ships. The cost of resoling began to rise rapidly, and Kevin's salary had been frozen for several years.

Kevin wore these shoes at home, too, day in and day out, and I was so tired of looking at them. He'd usually decide he should get a new pair about two days before he had to hop back on a plane. So we'd spend the entire next day searching for appropriate shoes, rushing them to a shoe repair shop, explaining to the repairman what had to be done, recovering from the sticker shock and hurrying back to pick them up before having to leave for the airport the next day. What had happened to the relaxing family time we were supposed to have together before Kevin left for a month at sea?

Jimmy, one of our church elders, who was also an evangelist, gave an amazing workshop on spiritual warfare while Kevin was at sea. Afterward I noticed him praying over a friend of mine while she was sitting down with both her legs straight out in front of her. He reached down and pulled on one of her feet.

One day while Kevin was still at sea, it struck me that the whole situation of having to find special shoes for Kevin and have them adjusted was just another way the devil was stealing from us. Time, money and joy were being sucked down the drain by what seemed like just one small issue of normal everyday life. Well, I wasn't going to fall for that anymore. We were going to keep our money, have our family time together, not be stressed by rushing around town trying to get all these things done on a deadline, and bonus: I wasn't going to have to look at those plain black shoes for the next 50 years. I was putting my foot down. So Kevin could put his down.

The scene I'd witnessed after the spiritual warfare seminar had been tugging at my mind all this time, so I asked Jimmy what it was I'd observed him doing to my friend's leg. He said, "Oh, she was having some back problems and asked for prayer. I had her sit with her hips flat against the chair back and put her legs out. It was obvious that one leg was slightly shorter than the other so I just prayed over it, and God grew it out to match the other. It's the easiest thing in the world to pray for — just a little faith and it's done."

"Next time you do one of those workshops, please make sure Kevin's going to be home. And don't leave until you've prayed over his left leg, OK?"

"You got it."

Woo-hoo! I could hardly wait. The next week I was walking through a department store, emphasis on *through* (remember the frozen salary), when my peripheral vision caught just a glimpse of a pair of men's shoes that stopped me short. I went back for a closer look. They were gorgeous driving mocs, the sexiest pair of men's shoes I'd ever laid eyes on. There was only one pair left. It was in Kevin's size. And they were half off. It was a sign. There is absolutely no way to have the sole raised on a driving moc.

Those mocs sat in Kevin's closet for a couple of months. Then Jimmy scheduled another spiritual warfare workshop — for the night Kevin was due to get home. Exhausted as he always was on returning, he was determined not to miss this special teaching. So we sped home from the airport. Kevin showered and changed clothes, then we rushed back out the door.

"Wait! Why are you wearing your work shoes? Honey, you need to wear those driving mocs I bought you."

"But I'll be walking in circles, and my back will twist."

"You'll be sitting down 90% of the time. You'll be fine. The point is to wear them as a statement of faith because tonight your left leg is going to grow out to the same length as the right one."

"OK, let's do it."

So off we went. I didn't get near as much out of the workshop that night as the first one. I was distracted by my sexy husband in driving mocs and no socks instead of white work socks and chunky looking black runners. When the teaching was over, I grabbed Jimmy and reminded him Kevin needed his leg lengthened.

"Sure, no problem." Two minutes and a prayer later, Jimmy declared it a done deal. I had just watched a leg get an inch and a half longer. Wow.

"Now," I asked, "Could you make both legs about four inches longer?" Kevin was about 5'10" and Jimmy, at 6'4", thought that was hilarious. I'd been saving that joke for months.

Leaving church, I asked Kevin how his leg felt.

"Kind of weird, but then it felt weird anyway, with no raised sole or heel lift."

We stopped to gas up, and Kevin hopped out of the truck and ran in to pay. Half way back from the cashier, he stopped cold and shouted, "Whoah!"

I stuck my head out the window to see what was happening.

"This is what it feels like to walk normally!" He walked a straight line that night and every day after and never had another problem — except for the expense of having the extra thick sole removed from his riding boots.

We'd been assured the 1992 back surgery would last five years, but possibly as many as ten, depending on the care taken. Kevin passed away 23 years after that surgery, and thanks to God lengthening his leg, he never had another issue with his back.

Miracle #5: leg grown out, no more back problems or related expenses, and best of all, I got to pick out his shoes.

Why didn't we think to ask the Lord to straighten the foot and reshape the lower leg at the same time? It kept Kevin from skiing and snowboarding. We "have not because we ask not," and that's the truth.

> ...call the elders of the church to pray over
> him and anoint him with oil in the name
> of the Lord. And the prayer offered in faith
> will restore the one who is sick.
> The Lord will raise him up. If he has
> sinned, he will be forgiven.
> – James 5:14,15 BSB

—&—

God does not waste our experiences. He turns them all, good and bad, to ultimate good for us, and for others. Is your healing only for yourself? No, just as He gives you financial blessings so that you can bless others, He heals you and proves to others He still heals today. Like anything else, it's easier to have faith for healing when you've experienced or witnessed healing yourself. (Thomas wasn't the only doubter.)

I had done it before, laid on hands and seen healing occur, but it was usually with a group. The day came, though, when it all fell into place. A man had asked for ministry from my cell group. When we were just talking, visiting, getting to know him, he mentioned he had one leg shorter than the other, and it was causing some back problems. Sound familiar? I knew I had finally met my now-or-never moment. If I wasn't obedient in that moment, my ministry would die before it was born.

I jumped up, repeating what Jimmy had said before praying over Kevin's leg, "That's the easiest thing in the world to pray for." I commanded his leg, and watched it grow out before my eyes.

Miracle #6: Another back healed.

Miracle #7: Ministry launched.

And these signs will accompany those who
believe: In My name they will...
lay their hands on the sick, and they will be made well.
– Mark 16:17,18 BSB

CURED OF THE INCURABLE

Reprinted from *Disarming Deadly Doctrines: Stop Sickness in its Tracks with Head-Smacking Revelations of God's Will*, Book One in the Head-Smacker Series by Kemala B. Tribe

"I've never seen anybody this bad. It's going to kill you, and it's going to kill you soon!" That's what the sleep lab technician told me after the obvious diagnosis of sleep apnea. I was waking myself up every five seconds to take a breath, and the tech told me he'd never seen a case as bad as mine. There was no cure, only the CPAP machine that creates positive air pressure to keep your airway from collapsing while you sleep. It was my only hope, he said.

Three years I'd gone without a decent night's sleep. It affected every area of my life. I could fall asleep on the dais during church, in front of everyone. Driving was a nightmare. Needless to say my temper was short, and my relationships with my husband and my son were suffering. I remember asking the Lord to remove my rage, lying that I'd read my Bible every day if He did. (Note to all: God doesn't need or want you to try to earn his blessings.) He took the rage, but I'm not going to tell you how many days in a row I read my Bible before failing grossly.

"As to the sleep apnea, I craved junk food for instant energy, and became addicted to drive-thrus. I would drive fifteen miles to a pick-up window rather than make something healthy at home. That addiction led to more health problems. I really had no idea how much the apnea was impacting my life, because it had become my normal.

I gave the CPAP machine my best shot, even praying for help from heaven, but the dry air burned my mouth and throat, and the mask made me claustrophobic. I finally couldn't keep the panic down, and came up out of the bed clawing that mask off.

"You HAVE to wear this!" The tech was truly concerned, but I knew somebody that could fix me without any machine.

The technician didn't have a very supportive response to my faith stance. "Oh, don't give me that! My daddy was a Baptist missionary, and I've heard all that before. God helps those that help themselves, and you have to use this CPAP, or you won't live much longer." I wanted to tell him that was a lie from the pit of hell — God wants us to fully rely on Him and lean not on our own understanding. Maybe I was just too tired to argue.

"Just call my husband to pick me up, please. Don't worry about me. I'll be healed Sunday morning."

I pulled my pastor aside thirty-two hours later, told her what was going on, and that I wasn't leaving church until I was healed. I'd stay all day, all week if necessary. So at the end of the service, she told everyone I was coming down front for healing and invited anyone that needed healing to join me. The pastor didn't pray over us — we were on our own in front of the Throne of Grace.

I didn't beg God, and I didn't try to make a deal — I'd learned that lesson. To be honest, I wasn't even reverent. I stood at the altar, arms crossed, and took my case to the Creator of the Universe. "The Bible says it was accomplished 2000 years ago, that it's Your will. If the Bible says it, You said it, and it's impossible for You to lie. So You don't have any choice but to heal me right now. I'm writing a check on my heavenly account as a joint heir with Christ for healing of sleep apnea. I'm coming boldly before your throne, and I'm not leaving until I know I'm healed."

By the time I felt my lungs open up, everyone else had left the altar. I don't know about them, but I was healed. I was cured of the incurable. Who can do that? Nobody but the Living God. And He loves you just as much as He loves me.

Did I really have to wait until Sunday morning to receive my healing? No. It just seemed like the easiest way, with my support system lifting me up in prayer and wonderful music to carry me into the throne room. But could I have gone into prayer or praise alone with the same results? Absolutely. You can receive your healing right now, right where you are, reading this book on a bus headed in to work, in the hospital, in bed at night with your spouse bugging you to turn off the light, or at the beach with the sun that God created just for you pounding down.

I'm still kicking myself, though, for not asking for more that Sunday morning. Ask big.

> So let us come boldly to the throne of our gracious God. There we will receive his mercy, and we will find grace to help us when we need it most.
> – Hebrews 4:16 NLT

"HERE, SMELL THIS!"

Where is that odor coming from? I have a keen sense of smell, but there weren't even any roses growing on adjacent properties, so it wasn't coming from outside. I'd been working hard all day, so… Nonetheless, the distinctive scent of roses was clear, and though it may make me one in a million, I don't even like roses. In fact, I can't use any cosmetics or toiletries containing essential oil of rose — I react badly to it. Still, off and on for months, usually when getting getting ready for bed, I smelled roses.

A month or so later, climbing into the car to go to a healing conference with a friend, I smelled the horrible, sharp odor of urine. It made my eyes burn, it was so strong. Now, I knew my friend had bladder issues, and I was praying she got healed at the conference. But she had never smelled like this.

I pointedly observed her husband in the car, and at the conference, other people we were around, but nobody took a step back, sniffed, wrinkled their nose or had any reaction at all to what I was enduring. I was the only one smelling it.

So I began to ask, *Lord, is there such a thing as SMELLING in the spirit? I've never heard of such a thing. It sounds crazy. We hear Your voice, and feel Your presence. I've heard of those who can see angels and who see demons with their claws in people. You proved to me we can taste You.* So I guess it would make sense that we could smell in the spirit, too — I've just never heard of it. And, gotta be honest, if You'd given me a choice of senses to use in the spirit realm, smell probably wouldn't have been my first choice.*

It was a large conference — probably three thousand people in attendance. The third night, during healing prayer, I was seated about four rows down and across the aisle from my friend with the bladder issue. And I smelled it. That's when I knew. It was a demon and it had been cast out of her. The odor was very strong even though I was probably 20-30 feet from my friend, and the venue had very strong fans blowing cold air. The smell came and went for several minutes, giving me the impressions the demon was darting about, running scared, trying to get back into my friend. But still, it sounded crazy even to myself to be smelling spiritual activity, and I didn't talk to anyone about it.

A couple of weeks later, I was watching a recording of an evangelist. After he spoke, he moved into the congregation and began praying over people. He was miked, so I could hear as he gave a word of knowledge to a woman on the front row. He went on to the next person, then stopped and stepped back to the woman who'd just received.

"You're being healed right now. God hasn't told me what you're being healed of…but you've been diagnosed with something quite serious, haven't you?"

She nodded. I couldn't hear what she said.

"Do you know how I know you're being healed?"

She shook her head.

"Because I smell roses."

Victory dance! I wasn't nuts, nor was I having mini-strokes. There really is such a thing as smelling in the spirit. It's useful in healing, discernment and words of knowledge. And for me, it had started with smelling roses from my own body.

My mother, when I told her about it, asked what I had been healed of.

"I have no idea, and I don't really care. I'll take it."

They have ears, but they hear not: noses have they, but they smell not:
– Psalm 115:6

*See Chapter 8 miracle account titled "Sweet"

SIN CAN'T STOP GOD

Partial reprint from *Disarming Deadly Doctrines: Stop Sickness in its Tracks with Head-Smacking Revelations of God's Will*, Book One in the Head-Smacker Series by Kemala B. Tribe

    When Kevin passed, I was eventually alone in our hotel room – physically alone for the first time without a husband. My son and his girlfriend had gone for take-out, assuring me they wouldn't be more than thirty minutes. I began to shake with cold and shock, and my feet felt like blocks of ice. They were so cold they burned. I had socks, but I could only get one on. More than a year earlier I had twisted my hip joint, and I couldn't make that inward swinging motion with my leg necessary to put on a sock. Even sitting on the bed, I couldn't bend toward that right foot enough to get a sock on it. Cocooned under the covers, with extra blankets piled on top, my right foot still ached with the cold. So I threw off the covers and snarled at Jesus, "You want to be my husband? Fine. Then GET down here and put this sock on for me because that's what Kevin would do." I was riled up. I never for a moment thought that God TOOK my husband, but I was mad that He didn't tell Kevin to come back for my sake.

    So there I was, angry at God, cursing Him, absolutely in a state of sin and not even caring that I was – not a repentant bone to be found in my body. What was the Lord's response? He healed my hip. Right there, sitting alone on the side of a hotel bed, nobody else around to pray over me. I hadn't even asked. He just met my need. He healed me so that I got my sock on without pain that night and every time I've wanted socks on since. It's not that often, as I'm a southern girl, and barefoot is a state of being in the south. But up north here, I admit, socks can be needful. And He met my need.

    I was full of anger (which He sees as murder), but His heart was still to heal me. That's how much, how deep, and how unconditional His love is for us. Sin cannot stop his love. Sin cannot stop His healing.

Their sins and lawless acts I will remember no more.
- Hebrews 10:17 NIV

– 5 –

PROVISION
Feeding the Flock

You may never know that Jesus is all you need, until Jesus is all you have.
— Corrie Ten Boom

Those who are readiest to trust God without other evidence than His Word always receive the greatest number of visible evidences of His love.
— Charles C.G. Trumbull

Please sir, I want some more.
— Charles Dickens' Oliver Twist

Supply, just in the nick of time, is not necessarily a miracle, but often the result of God rebuking the devourer for tithers, as promised, and/or the result of the law of "seed, time and harvest." Other times, it may be a miracle, like my friend's dead car working when she needed it to because of her trust in God, then dying again as she pulled back into the driveway.

Where financial supply is needed, I highly recommend tithing, and tithe your first fruits. Never try to tithe from what you have left over at the end of the month. That's putting God last in your life. It will get you nowhere. Remember that your heart follows where you put your treasure. God does love a cheerful giver, but He tells you to test him when it comes to tithing and see if it pays off. It will. You can't outgive the owner of everything. And when you see it pays off, you'll become cheerful! You'll find it's so much fun to give.

Proof of God's Will

> Bring all the tithes (the tenth) into the storehouse, so that there may be food in My house, and test Me now in this," says the Lord of hosts, "if I will not open for you the windows of heaven and pour out for you [so great] a blessing until there is no more room to receive it.
>
> - Malachi 3:10 AMP

> But seek first the kingdom of God and his righteousness, and all these things will be added to you.
>
> - Matthew 6:33 ESV

> For it was I, the LORD your God, who rescued you from the land of Egypt. Open your mouth wide, and I will fill it with good things.
>
> - Psalm 81:10 NLT

> The blessing of the LORD establishes wealth, and difficulty does not accompany it.
>
> - Proverbs 10:22 ISV

> A generous soul will prosper, and he who refreshes another will himself be refreshed.
>
> - Proverbs 11:25 BSB

> But remember the Lord your God is the one who makes you wealthy. He's confirming the promise which he swore to your ancestors. It's still in effect today.
>
> - Deuteronomy 8:18 GWT

TUNA CASSEROLE

As a child I barely knew there was a world outside my hometown in South Georgia. But the day came when that world became very real. My dad was developing a subdivision, building the houses under a federal program that ended abruptly, rather than being phased out. So one Friday, Daddy came home and gave Mama the good news that we could start building our new house, and Monday at lunchtime he walked in the door and broke the news that his business, and income, simply didn't exist anymore.

We moved to central Florida. It was horrible, leaving home. Eventually I adjusted, though *eventually* felt like a long, long time. I was thirteen.

Starting up a business from scratch in a new state takes time, and financially, it was a real struggle for my dad to make ends meet. For a while, he worked as a sub-trade contractor. Those were very long, very physical days, in tropical heat. And my twelve-year-old brother worked right alongside him, all summer long. He worked like a full-grown man and never complained.

Meanwhile, Mom was being as frugal as possible. I particularly remember her tuna casserole. It was delicious. One cup of macaroni, one can of tuna, one small block of cream cheese, one can of soup, and a few minor ingredients — and it was one of my favorite meals.

Do you know that ten years later, my husband loved that recipe, too. We would make a double recipe, and eat nothing with it because it was all we wanted. We would continue to pick at that 9x12 pan all evening until it was empty. Are you hearing me? There were two of us, and we'd eat a double recipe.

But back when I was thirteen, when my family was in need, the four of us, two of whom were doing manual labor all day in the blistering sun, ate a single recipe only. And there'd be two big helpings left to fill the men's lunch boxes the next day.

I was young and now I am old, yet I have never seen the righteous forsaken or their children begging bread.
- Psalm 37:25 NIV

THE CHECK IS IN THE MAIL

Crunch time. The house of cards was about to fall. And being in the same house with my husband that week was like trying to share a den with a bear.

We had rededicated our lives to Christ that year, and though we seemed to be on the same page when we emailed back and forth ship-to-shore, when Kevin came home from sea, he was…still Kevin. I was home being spoon-fed knowledge of God by friends, while Kevin was off at sea with a bunch of scandihooligans. In my heart I knew he'd be home for a while soon, so that God could establish a foundation in him, and he could begin to renew his mind.

The company wanted my husband, who was Chief Officer at the time, and the captain, to sign paperwork stating certain tests related to environmental safety had been conducted, when they had not, and do so on an ongoing basis. Sure, the paperwork and the testing that governmental agencies were now requiring were over the top to the point of being nonsensical. Plus, Kevin was already working on about 2 hours sleep per night when on the Gulf Coast, and certainly didn't need more tests to conduct or more paperwork to fill out. But shore management had picked the wrong officers to try to manhandle. The captain had been master of Greenpeace's Rainbow Warrior, and Kevin was a Christian. Neither were going to lie, and neither were going to put their licenses on the line for a paycheck.

Kevin kept telling me he wanted to quit. I kept telling him to bide his time a little longer. Sure enough, the company came up with some excuse to dismiss him, but because he hadn't quit, Kevin got an extra month's pay as severance. He wasn't the least bit concerned about being jobless — he was highly employable.

Uh-huh. Remember I said that I knew he was going to be home for a while? I welcomed that, but we were already barely scraping by. Real estate rich and cash poor, Kevin's salary had been frozen for five years and I was new at real estate sales and mortgage brokering. The severance pay only lasted a few weeks, and just for fun, the vacancy rate on our rentals soared. But Kevin was sending out resumes and getting to know God.

Still, he would periodically freak out as our income shrank with more vacancies. My mortgage broker business, which I was just beginning to get a handle on, suddenly dried up. It was tied directly to my dad's home improvement business, which experienced a sudden downturn. What was going on?

"What are we going to do?" Kevin would say.

I wasn't worried. "God's got this. No need to stress."

Kevin sat at the desk, figures in front of him, looking panicked. He'd sent out dozens of resumes with no promising responses.

Meanwhile, we were fellowshipping, reading our Bibles, renewing our minds, becoming closer as a family.

"What are we going to do?"

Bills would come in again, credit cards would max out. Everything got paid — I don't know how. There we were in that beautifully appointed historic home, and more than once I made a phone call, "Mama, can we come to dinner?"

And Kevin would freak out. At that time, I could still calm him, "Honey, don't worry. God is dealing with it. He's got us." Then I would go into another room, hide behind the door and freak out myself. "Lord, what is the deal here? We're nearly out of time!"

And then it was the last day — the last day before we had to get nearly $6,000 into the bank or we were going to miss every mortgage payment on every property, including our home. Kevin was fit to be tied. He snapped at everything I said, he paced and railed. For me the stress wasn't the financial situation, it was the state Kevin was in. It was late afternoon and the phone rang, in the middle of harsh words being flung around.

I snatched it up, "WHAT?"

A friend said, "Ummm…what's going on?"

"This man is impossible today. We have to have a bunch of money in the bank tomorrow or we're going to default on everything, and he's so stressed out I can't live with him."

"We're on our way."

We all sat down at the kitchen table, and they explained that we were now God's children. We were the bride of Christ. Our debt was His debt. They sent Kevin to write down a list of every debt. We set that list in the middle of the table and prayed over it. We gave it to the Lord. We cast that care upon Jesus. Now it was His problem, and we didn't have to worry about it anymore. Kevin was relaxed and happy the rest of the night.

The next morning, I tested the waters and found him still calm. Then he said, "We're cleaning the office today."

"Oh. Honey, I'm sorry, but I have three appointments today."

"Well, you're going to have to reschedule, because we're cleaning the office today."

"But people are counting on me. You know, the deal where I'm representing both parties AND writing the mortgage? The buyers are really feeling the time pressure, plus, the faster I get this deal through the faster I get paid."

"I understand that, but we're not doing anything else until this office is cleaned."

Normally, he would never get away with being that…we'll just call it insistent, and truthfully, I'd never seen him like that before. And man, was I dreading dealing with that office. But in the interest of not having a day like the one before, I agreed and rescheduled my meetings. When Kevin said *clean,* he was referring to filing and dealing with a three-foot stack of mail. When Kevin was at sea, my daily responsibilities were like that of any single parent with a job and a business to run. So when it came to mail, if it didn't look familiar, I just tossed it on the couch in the office. And filing became yet another pile. But if that's what it took to appease the savage beast, then I'd grit my teeth and deal with it.

It was grueling. About 4:40, I had gone into the kitchen when I heard Kevin yell.

"Praise God! Praise God! Kemala — come look at this!" I smiled. God had us. *Told 'ya.* I leaned against the doorway of the office.

"What did you find?"

"Two checks. I don't know why there are two, but the life insurance policy — the one my dad bought me when I was a baby — the company was bought out. They paid us a dividend. There's a total of nearly SIX THOUSAND DOLLARS here. They were in the pile on the couch. Been there since July."

"Four months. Good thing I didn't open them back in the summer. We'd have another really beautiful antique."

He kissed me and ran out the door — just fifteen minutes to get the deposit in. Later he told me he had rolled the windows down, yelling "Praise God! Thank you, Jesus!" All the way to the bank.

Yeah. Did I mention it was a small town?

> I will answer them before they even call to me.
> While they are still talking about their needs,
> I will go ahead and answer their prayers!
> – Isaiah 65:24 NLT

THE WEEK FROM HEAVEN

After the checks were taken to the bank, bills continued to get paid, but we really didn't know how. You know that scripture that says God works in mysterious ways? I think that's the real meaning — He gets things done but you have no idea how it happened.

We were still in the same boat — 80% vacancy rate. We put the properties on the market, and we were selling my fully loaded Grand Caravan. But we had no bites on anything, not even nibbles. It was as if our ads were invisible. Obviously, we needed renters if we wanted a decent price on rental property. But people don't want to rent if their potential home is for sale. They're afraid they'll get kicked out, plus there's the pain of having potential buyers wanting to view their home. So that was a Catch 22 situation. And Kevin was still looking for a job. He'd had no income for 4 1/2 months. Nonetheless, whatever came in, we tithed on.

The reason for selling everything, though, wasn't impending poverty. It was that we'd finally found our church — the one God wanted us in. After visiting every local church, we'd "happened" into this one when we'd gone to Atlanta for my cousin's wedding. It felt like home. And it was 250 miles away. We weren't in a hurry, but we were preparing.

We'd been going back and forth most weekends, staying with friends in the area. We'd leave home on Friday if we'd made plans with them, or Saturday, go to church with them on Sunday morning, then attend "our" church on Sunday night. We'd get home anytime from 1:00-3:00 a.m. Monday morning.

This one particular Sunday, a favorite evangelist was to speak at a church in Smyrna — about 20 miles northwest of Atlanta, whereas. our church was about 30 miles southeast of Atlanta. We decided to go to Smyrna. We got up early to drive the 4+ hours and fought all the way. At one point, Kevin hit the brakes, U-turned, and headed home.

"Oh, so you're going to let the devil win?"

He hit the brakes again and headed for church. We decided silence was the best option.

When we arrived, the person we went to hear had cancelled. In his place, they had called in a young woman from their sister church in Detroit. I don't know what it was she said, but whatever it was, it was what my husband needed to hear. He was on fire. We didn't leave the church until after 3 p.m.

Of course, we were starving, and as we were finishing our meal at Morrison's Cafeteria, feeling fabulous, Kevin checked the time - 4:30 p.m. We just looked at each other, thinking the same thing. We jumped in the van, sped through Atlanta, and pulled into the parking lot just in time for the evening service. We could hear the praise music had already started.

Right behind us, speeding in almost to the point of squealing tires, was our pastor's son. He jumped out of his car, grabbing at papers that seemed determined to fly away, and said, "Hey guys, good to see you, can't talk. I'm preaching tonight and I'm running late. God completely changed my sermon about 4:30, so, see you after."

Again, Kevin and I just looked at each other. Then we burst out laughing. God is amazing.

Britt called this sermon The Channel, and said there was a channel, like a pipe, between you and God through which we communicate with Him. Sometimes that channel gets clogged by issues like fear, unbelief, unforgiveness. I think he pointed out seven potential blockages. He led the congregation through a prayer to clean every blockage out of that channel. I felt peace. He dismissed us, then said, "Oh! I forgot to say — once that channel is cleaned out, all the blessings God's been trying to get to you will come RUSHING through."

I left there knowing that the second sermon was for me. We drove home and got to bed about 4:00 a.m.

At 8:00 the phone rang.

"Hi, I'm calling from Rex, Georgia up near Covington."

Rex was nowhere near Covington. But Covington was where we were going to move, to go to the church God had for us. God was calling.

"Yes sir, what can I do for you?"

"My wife found the ad for your minivan, and it's exactly what she's been looking for — EXACTLY. I hope you still have it. She decided two months ago what she wanted, and we've looked everywhere. We've even had dealers looking. They said it didn't exist with that combination of colors and features, and that she should buy one that's close to what she wants. But she said, 'No, I know what I want, and I know God has it for me.'"

"You know, that ad has been up for about two months."

"Really? She's been looking and looking and didn't find it until last night."

"Well, we were up near Rex last night for church, but now we're about a 4-hour drive away. Can you wait until next weekend?"

Tuesday morning the phone started ringing. We filled two vacancies.

Wednesday morning the phone rang. It was the person God sent to buy the 4-plex.

Thursday morning — the buyer for the duplex, and a renter.

Friday morning came. The phone rang. It was the job Kevin had been wanting for the past 18 months — his number one choice of career moves.

I guess that channel got unblocked.

So they all ate and were filled, and they took up twelve baskets full of the fragments that remained.
- Matthew 14:20 NKJV

TWO-FOR-ONE SPECIAL

The time came to sell the house and move north for church. I would miss our beautiful turn-of-the-century home, but I was much more excited to start our new life right in the center of God's will. I've been known to say that getting me to WANT to leave that house is the real miracle.

The real estate broker I worked for suggested a price based on what he knew about similar houses, and I offered it at that price to somebody I knew was interested in an historic home. They didn't make an offer. So I listed it, and my broker had graciously cancelled all commission except the small amount that had to go to corporate. Filling out the listing agreement, which I had done so many times now with clients, took only minutes, and without any thought about it, I raised the price $30,000. Kevin signed it with me. It was amazing how little he stressed any more. He asked about the price.

I said, "I don't know. That's what came out of the pen."

"OK, cool."

When I handed it to my broker, he said, "What are you doing? That's not the price we talked about."

"No, but that's what I wrote." He looked baffled. "It's OK, that's what it'll sell for. It's a God thing."

He raised his eyebrows, but shrugged and let it go — for about a month. "Are you ready to lower the price now? You've hardly even shown it at that price."

"No, it'll sell, don't worry. It's a God thing." We did the same dance two weeks later. And a week after that.

One day he phoned to tell me there was a couple coming to town with cash to buy an historic home if they saw the right one. Otherwise, they'd move along to the next town.

"They actually called to enquire about the Jackson house, but I thought I'd drive them by yours, and if it interests her, we'll just come up to the door. So I wanted to give you a heads-up in case you need to get it ready for a showing."

That house was always ready for a showing. An hour later, there was a knock at the front door. Five minutes later, this lovely woman and I were discussing her rugs and which one would look better in which room. Full price, cash.

So then we had to see if we could buy the land we had fallen in love with near our new church. The strangest connection had come to light. The owner knew the friend we stayed overnight with when we went up to middle Georgia for church on the weekends. In fact, they had been in business together. The landowner handled the production end of things. The sales end was handled by — get this — my dad. This man had been in business with my dad, yet they'd never met. We wrote a very humble letter to this man, telling how we saw the land being used for the Kingdom of God, and apologizing for making such a low offer, but that it was all we could pay, and we completely understood if he rejected it. It was about 40% of his advertised price.

We got a letter back. He said it was an interesting offer, because it was exactly the amount he needed to pay off his debts and build a mission in Peru. He accepted our offer.

Looking back, I cannot explain how we came up with that offer. I remember Kevin saying, "That's all we have to work with for now." We never sat down together and figured out what we'd have after we closed the sale of our house. God had to have planted it in our brains because we were so surprised to find out at closing, that the check we left the attorney's office with was the exact amount we'd agreed to pay for the land, plus just enough to pay for the move.

---

*...for your Father knows what you
need before you ask Him.
– Matthew 6:8 BSB*

WHO'S YOUR DADDY?

During another renovation, years later, on the house I downsized to after my husband died, money eventually got tight, as it does with most every renovation. But supplies would show up. Once I asked how much a piece of culvert would cost. I wanted to enlarge the parking area for when my friends came for cell group and game night. The best price we could come up with, from a salvage yard, was three hundred seventy-five dollars.

"It'll wait," I told Terry, my reno guy.

A week later, somebody I'd never met slowed down as he was driving past my house and saw Terry working out front.

"Hey, Terry! Heard you need a piece of culvert. There's one in my front yard. Go get it."

He sped off. The next day Terry went to look at the culvert. It was the perfect diameter. It was the perfect length. It was free.

Things like that happened regularly, and the guys who worked for me began to expect it. I would just shrug and say, "I know who my Daddy is. He takes care of His kids."

Over time, I'd overhear things like, "Hey, where'd you find that part?"

"At the recycle depot, for $2."

"What? That's a $60 part — oh right. It's for Kemala."

In the beginning, those guys would just shake their heads like I was crazy when I'd say I relied on my heavenly Father. But with every deal, they got more and more curious about my God.

Every good and perfect gift is from above,
coming down from the Father of the heavenly lights,
who does not change like shifting shadows.
– James 1:17 NIV

COURT OF HEAVEN?

I asked my roofer-friend, "How much is the metal going to cost?"

"Twenty-five hundred, maybe three thousand, depending on the source. If I can get it for you at the discount place, I will. If not, it'll be about three thousand."

Good deal — much better than the $17k I would have to pay for a new metal roof under most circumstances. The guys were donating their labor. Amazing, right? But Terry was living in my guest bedroom, and he'd offered his buddy two days of free labor building his deck if he'd work two days with him putting on my roof.

I was headed for Georgia and expected to be away six weeks, so I left the house in their capable hands. I was gone for nearly six months.

About a week after I got home, I was looking over the pile of mail, and wondered why the bill from the building supply store was so thick. Shock — I was $7k in debt with no income to cover it. I was expecting $3k. How had this happened?

Turns out I had asked the wrong question. He gave me the correct information on the cost of the metal, I just hadn't asked the cost of all the other supplies needed to do the job — underlay, screws you never have to re-tighten, flashing, vents, etc… Everything is so expensive in Canada.

So I phoned my building supply store friend, explained, apologized, and told him I'd get something worked out. He wasn't happy.

Several weeks went by, and most of the time I didn't worry about it. But I'm human, and once in a while I'd stress over it. Then I'd remind myself that God would take care of me. When Kevin passed away, my first prayer had been that God not only go before me, but come behind me to clean up my messes because I knew I wouldn't always hear him, nor would I always be obedient. And this time my mess was financial.

My attorney, who had helped me with probate, phoned to say that the cabin, which I'd decided I couldn't keep, had sold. It had not been an easy decision. The bank had raised the mortgage payment, and that was the last straw, since now I'd be in a negative cash flow situation on that property. It already was slightly upside down, mortgage-wise. And without Kevin, I really didn't want to be a landlord. However, the lending rules had changed, and the banks would not provide a mortgage for the cabin due to the type of foundation. So any potential buyer would have to pay cash. At the time, with personal challenges I was facing, the sentimental value of the cabin and the fact that I really wanted to keep it for my son — well, I just couldn't face dealing with it myself. So I gave it back to the bank. I have sold many houses myself, but I just couldn't deal with the emotions I would have to face selling that cabin. Better to walk away. So the attorney's call was good news. I wouldn't make money on it, but I wouldn't go into the hole every month any longer. That was the last of the financial worries dealt with.

The next week the attorney phoned again.

"Kemala, I have something to tell you. Yesterday, when the buyer went before the foreclosure judge to pay for the cabin…

Oh no, what now?

…somebody else came in at the last moment, and offered more money. I have a check for roughly $16,000 for you. Would you like to pick it up? Or I could mail it to you.

The hardware store friend was very happy for me.

> Now to him who is able to do far more
> abundantly than all that we ask or think,
> according to the power at work within us,
> – Ephesians 3:20 ESV

ALWAYS ASK FOR MORE

I'd gone home to Georgia for about six months, spent time with family and made a couple of road trips to visit people I hadn't seen in years. But the primary reason behind the trip was to get our belongings out of storage. Paying storage fees for ten years wasn't smart, but there were family antiques involved and the tangible expressions of the years Kevin and I had spent traveling the world. There were a lot of bittersweet moments going through all the belongings. There was also a lot of sifting to be done. Damage by movers, items I'd long ago replaced, art I just didn't have room for in my new, smaller home all had to be dealt with. A lot of clothes had to be thrown out. There were boxes of 10+ year-old paperwork for the landfill… At the last moment, I gave in to the feeling I should haul those boxes back to Canada with me and sort through them at home. There was no telling what I might find.

On the day I decided to attack the boxes of paperwork, I was in for a big surprise. I came across the termination letter from that company that had fired Kevin for not doing something illegal. Renewed anger at the injustice flared in me as I read it. I'd had the same reaction when I phoned them after Kevin's death to check on a spouse's pension, and had been told that he'd worked for them 4 months shy of the requirement for receiving a pension — such a convenient time to fire him. I was gritting my teeth by the time I got to the bottom of the letter.

Then my eyes popped out. I read the final paragraph again.

I got the same man on the phone that had told me Kevin hadn't worked for them long enough to get a pension. He gave me his fax number. I sent him a copy of the letter, the last paragraph of which said, "Of course, you're fully vested, and will begin receiving pension payments one month after your sixtieth birthday."

Two days later I heard back from him with an offer, which I refused. I stood my ground. When it was over, they paid me Kevin's full pension from the day he turned sixty to the day he died, and a spouse's half-pension backdated to Kevin's death — a nice lump sum unexpected windfall. The best news was the pension payments, modest though they are, are for life. I remembered the monologue I'd prayed a couple of months earlier.

Father, I'm so grateful for the way You've taken care of me since Kevin died. If it hadn't been for everything you did when Kevin first came back to Canada, I wouldn't have the pension from the ferry now. And you've done exactly what I prayed for — You've gone before me and made a way where there was none, and you've fixed everything I messed up. So I don't want you to think I'm not grateful. I'm just wondering…I'd love to have a little more wiggle room in my budget. I have no idea how you would do it, but I know there are no restrictions on what you can do. An extra $250 a month would mean that when a friend phoned, I wouldn't have to figure out if I can afford to go to lunch or a movie. And socializing is important to me these days, since I have so much time alone. And gifts — You know how I love to give gifts — maybe $300 would be a better figure. Yes, $300 would — well, let's say $350, because you know how I love to buy Christian books and study materials. Do you think you could find another $350 per month for me somewhere? I feel selfish asking, but I know you want me to ask, so there it is.

The pension God uncovered redeemed all Kevin's hard work for that ungrateful, underhanded foreign company. And it gave me $350 every month for life. I intend to live a very long time.

```
Let them shout for joy and be glad,
   Who favor my righteous cause;
And let them say continually, "Let
       the LORD be magnified,
Who has pleasure in the prosperity of His servant."
             - Psalm 35:27 NKJV
```

– 6 –

RELATIONSHIPS
Remaining in Love

> The best thing to hold onto in life is each other.
> - Audrey Hepburn

> The best and most beautiful things in the world cannot be seen or even heard, but must be felt with the heart.
> - Helen Keller

> For better or for worse…
> - Kevin and Kemala Tribe

Miracles are often not cut and dried when it comes to relationships. Maybe you can't even call them miracles, because they rely on two people both obeying God, or at least one of them experiencing a heart change. As you will read in the next chapter, a heart change can be stunning and sudden. All you need to do is give God permission. He is a God of restoration, and Christianity is all about relationships, so give Him an inch. Ask Him into your relationships and watch Him do the miraculous.

Proof of God's Will

> Behold, how good and pleasant it is when brothers dwell in unity!
> - Psalm 133:1 NIV

> One who has unreliable friends soon comes to ruin, but there is a friend who sticks closer than a brother.
> - Proverbs 18:24 NIV

> If one falls, the other can help his friend get up. But how tragic it is for the one who is [all] alone when he falls. There is no one to help him get up.
> - Ecclesiastes 4:10 GWT

> You are my friends if you do what I command you. I do not call you servants anymore, because a servant doesn't know what his master is doing. I have called you friends, because I have made known to you everything I have heard from my Father.
> - John 15:14-15 CSB

RIGHT ON TIME

We moved four-and-a-half hours north of my home town to become part of the church God had called us to. We'd been visiting there for over a year, driving back and forth most weekends, and it was wonderful to have gotten to know some people there before moving. But that had been primarily confined to visiting after the service on Sunday nights. We usually attended a different church on Sunday mornings, with the friends we stayed over with on Saturday nights — it just seemed like the right thing to do. But we realized after we moved, that all these people who'd been so willing to visit after church and were so welcoming when we arrived with our moving van, had their own lives.

They had to go to work every day. Their kids had activities they had to be chauffeured to and from. They had extended family to spend time with, routines and schedules to be adhered to, and good friends they already had plans with. The inundation of friends we were expecting, perhaps subconsciously, just didn't happen.

Even realizing it takes time to become part of other people's lives, it was disappointing. I felt especially lonely when Kevin went off to sea, having left my family in the southern part of the state. But there was a silver lining — Christian television.

In those days, there was no Christian television available in my little home town, and I soaked it up. All day every day I was glued to the television. It was so refreshing. I learned the different personalities, discerning who spoke truth and who I wanted to avoid. Jesus said He came to set us free, so it was usually easy to tell who spoke for Him.

The day came, though, when I had to say, "Lord, I really need a friend. Somebody to spend time with, do girl stuff with, talk on the phone with." That was a Friday.

Sunday night we celebrated our pastor's birthday after church, and two different young women spent the entire party talking with me. We became instant friends. I was never lonely in Georgia again.

A friend loves at all times, and a brother
is born for a time of adversity.
— Proverbs 17:17 NIV

PRAYER'S PAYOFF

There was a season when life was routine. We'd built our house in central Georgia, we were established in a church family and a homeschool group, and Kevin was working month-on month-off overseas. Our son and I would miss him and look forward to his arrival every time, but when he got home, he was…well… himself. My son and I had a way of doing things, and Kevin disrupted it. More than that, he was still in Captain mode, and I was used to making all the decisions. I was the teacher, but the Principal tried to take over the classroom when he was home. His inner accountant questioned every receipt. Since I was no longer traveling with him overseas, I no longer knew the people he worked with nor understood his new work, so we couldn't really talk about how he spent half his life. All that and much more — we were just not meshing. The time we had together was abbreviated due to his travel days and his level of exhaustion when he arrived home.

The one thing we seemed to have in common was that we knew where each other's buttons were. So we would look forward to every reunion, then were disappointed. Most of his time at home every other month, Kevin and I picked at each other. KJ and I breathed a sigh of relief every time we dropped him off at the airport.

Then one day he came home and seemed different. He didn't snap; he didn't raise his voice; he asked before he acted; his tone was kinder, gentler overall. He was tender toward us. We felt loved, validated — special to him. About ten days after arriving home, he was going through some bills while I was making supper, and I interrupted him with a question. He snapped at me! Where had that come from? It wasn't that we didn't know how to be kind, we were just locked into a certain cycle of act/react habits.

I was just about to jump down his throat, when I caught myself. *No, he's been so nice the entire time he's been home. I'll answer nicely and see what happens.* I could feel his realization and pause before he spoke again. He apologized later and thanked me for not reacting in kind.

We had the most wonderful time together, enjoying each other's company and family time together every day. KJ and I began to dread the looming departure date. The drive to the airport was a sad affair. KJ and I were in tears. I finally broached the subject.

"Kevin, how is it that we've had such a wonderful time together this past month? We're missing you already."

"I don't know. Maybe it's because the whole time I was away, I prayed about being kinder to my family."

Maybe this doesn't seem like a miracle to you, but it sure did to my son and me.

> A gentle answer turns away anger, but
> a harsh word stirs up wrath.
> – Proverbs 15:1 CSB

– 7 –

BINDING UP THE BROKEN HEARTS
Nobody Knows but Jesus

In three words I can sum up everything I've learned about life: it goes on.

- Robert Frost

Someday you're gonna look back on this moment of your life as such a sweet time of grieving. You'll see that you were in mourning and your heart was broken, but your life was changing.

- Elizabeth Gilbert

Proof of God's Will

"The Lord is close to the brokenhearted and saves those who are crushed in spirit."

- Psalm 34:18 NIV

He heals the brokenhearted And binds up their wounds [healing their pain and comforting their sorrow].

- Psalm 147:3 AMP

Christ died for us while we were still sinners. This demonstrates God's love for us.

- Romans 5:8 GWT

"Do not be anxious about anything, but in every situation, by prayer and petition, with thanksgiving, present your requests to God. And the peace of God, which transcends all understanding, will guard your hearts and your minds in Christ Jesus.

- Philippians 4:6-7 NIV

"Come to me, all you who are weary and burdened, and I will give you rest."

- Matthew 11:28 NIV

Never will I leave you; never will I forsake you.

- Hebrews 13:5 NIV

OUR BEST LAID PLANS

For eighteen years, Kevin and I fought US Immigration. You'd have thought Kevin was from Libya or something. No, he was Canadian — he'd just had a misspent youth. Meanwhile, he was rising to the position of Captain of the largest, newest, highest-tech drillship in the world, but Immigration was unimpressed. I wanted to raise my son in my home town because my husband's career kept him away half the time. But because we'd been honest on the Immigration paperwork, every time my brilliant, godly husband went to work, I had no idea if he'd be allowed to come home. I resented that the country I loved so much wanted me to choose between it, including my birth family, and my husband.

Sometimes the stress was nearly unbearable, but we did eventually find a work-around and an ally or two within the bureaucracy. Nonetheless, the day finally came when we had to either put up or shut up. So Kevin submitted an application for permanent residency. By that time at God's direction, we'd moved to central Georgia to become part of the church God had prepared for us, so everything went through the Atlanta INS office. It was a grueling, stressful process.

Kevin was at sea when our son and I stopped at the mailbox as we were leaving for Wednesday night church. The official envelope felt electrified. I opened it.

The twenty-minute drive to church was all on autopilot. I was in a numb state of shock and disbelief. Tears kept running down my face during the teaching. Our pastors weren't there that night, so as soon as the service ended, I grabbed their son, who'd been speaking, and an elder-friend and dragged them into a private office to show them the letter.

But what were they supposed to do?

How was I going to tell Kevin? He had to be able to enter the U.S. or his career might be over. We weren't even making ends meet at that time, so how were we supposed to support two households? And how would that work with our marriage, anyway? And GOD!

How could He have let this happen? He had told me He would take care of this. He'd given me Isaiah 33:20-24 and I'd stood on that message for years — that He would give us a peaceful home, one where the warships could not sail, where HE would be our Lawgiver. I'd believed Him, and He'd let me down. Never mind that every time I thought about that scripture, I'd hear, "Kemala, I never said it would be in the States." No, no, that was the enemy trying to dissuade me from my faith stance. It had to be, right? Now I was scared, angry, heartbroken, confused, and I couldn't let my child see any of it.

At home, I told my son I didn't feel well and went to bed. I curled up in a ball and sobbed with angry, bitter tears at the injustice of it all, at the years wasted trying to carve out a home, at wanting to raise my son in the South where respect and manners and family still mattered — at trusting God. And the biggest, immediate problem kept resounding in my head like a foghorn — how am I going to tell Kevin?

His work was incredibly intense. He had to stay focused. A distraction like this could be disastrous, literally. And yet he had to be told in time for the office to change his flights, because if he landed on U.S. soil, he was headed to jail, court, and deportation. It would be on his record, and it would make the whole situation worse, if that was even possible. How could I tell him?

Hopelessness was trying to set up camp in my heart. I knew I needed some support, but I also knew it was very, very important to watch my words — those I spoke and even those I heard. I had no strength to overcome the cries of those who loved me and would share their dismay with me. So I emailed the only two people I knew that would instantly go into warfare mode and speak only words of faith. Then I crawled back in bed for another crying jag and the escape of a little sleep.

And so it went all night and all the next day — cycles of railing at God, crying, napping fitfully, checking email. And every time I checked email, my friends sent me EXACTLY what I needed to be reminded of at that very moment. They were listening to Holy Spirit, the Comforter, supplying sanity and love.

But how was I going to tell Kevin?

Finally, that second night, having so much anger toward the Creator of the Universe began to feel a little dangerous. I was exhausted by torrential emotions, and needed real rest. I gave up.

Lord, I can admit at this point, that you have a plan. But honestly, right now, I couldn't care less what that plan is. You didn't do what I was believing you to do, and I'm so angry at you. I know I shouldn't be, but I don't know how to NOT be. So, I'm going to go to sleep. And you're just going to have to deal with all this while I sleep. I don't know how you're going to do it, but hey, you're God. So, goodnight.

I was out like a light. The next thing I knew, beautiful sunlight was streaming in, and something else was different, too. I couldn't identify it at first, then I realized — I was grinning from ear to ear! I was so excited to find out what God had up his sleeve, I could hardly contain myself. I jumped out of bed and headed for the computer to tell Kevin we were about to have another adventure with God.

Kevin flew into his home country of Canada, and from that point, miracle after miracle confirmed that God was going before us, preparing the way. He provided free lodging in the city, friends to stay with later, the additional income we needed, divine appointments. There was no opportunity to doubt that we were walking in God's plan for our lives. God was with us every step of the way, and it felt good.

...Weeping may last for the night, But a
shout of joy *comes* in the morning.
- Psalm 30:5 NASB

THE BOULDER, THE TREE AND THE HEARTACHE

It's difficult to part with a home that you've put your heart into and that holds so many memories, but after my husband's death, it was necessary. I had to downsize to eliminate that monthly mortgage payment. Knowing that no matter how much I spent on a house, I'd still want to tear walls out, replace every surface, and otherwise put my mark on it, I asked to see the cheapest homes on the market.

After having done at least ten renovations of properties in various states of repair, disuse, even decay, I was not frightened away by the bad vinyl siding job I parked in front of that day in June. This was my second look, and I'd brought my favorite renovation guy with me. He rolled his eyes at me as we walked through the front door into the lingering odors of pot smoke and last night's cabbage with underlying notes of urine and rot. From what I'd heard, every teenager and addict in town had lived in this rental house at one time or another, and despite it having been renovated only six years earlier, every surface appeared to have had decades of abuse.

When you opened the front door, the view was through an archway, directly to the kitchen sink. Job one: either the sink or the archway had to move.

"So, what do you like about this house?" Terry the reno guy asked.

"The price."

He gave an amused snort, then, "Anything else?"

"Not much yard work." The house was close to the road, and backed up to a steep hill that could be left natural. "There is a reason I'm going to make an offer, but I have to show you." I used to complain to Kevin that we didn't have any big rocks at either the cabin we first lived in or the house on the cliff. It seemed every property on this island had big, beautiful rocks but ours. Kevin offered to have some brought in, but it seemed a silly thing to spend money on. Still, I love the serenity of rocks and moss. It was not something I would miss out on at this house, though.

To Terry I said, "When we first moved here, I explored the island, trying to drive every road. And on this street here, I found the most beautiful thing — an enormous cedar tree straddling a boulder. How it ever grew there I can't even imagine. I picked Kevin up from the ferry and took him to see it. For the first four or five years we lived here, whenever we were in this area, we'd visit that huge boulder with the tree growing around it. Then one day it just wasn't there. We drove back and forth, up and down the road, wondering how we could miss it, and finally realized it just wasn't there anymore. We assumed that it had been deemed dangerous and somebody had cut it down."

I ushered Terry into the laundry room, trying to tread lightly — it was one source of the rotting wood smell — and out the back door. Angels sang every time I opened that door. The sight was breathtaking. Mountainous boulders braced each other on the hillside I knew I'd seldom climb. And the one closest to the house split the trunk of a towering cedar.

"The owner barged this house over from the mainland, and set it on this piece of land in front of the cedar-boulder Kevin and I loved. My house is why we couldn't see it from the street."

The first time the realtor showed me this house, I'd been floored when I stepped onto the back stoop. "Now I understand, Lord." He'd saved the cedar tree and boulders for my first home without Kevin, so I'd know this house was my gift from Him.

> I love the Lord, because He hears My
> voice and my supplications.
> – Psalm 116:1 NASB

A VISION OF ENCOURAGEMENT

"Oh. You're here." I was only mildly surprised, which of itself was surprising — since he'd been dead nearly five years. He was laying on my bed — I say mine, because he'd never lived in this house and I'd put our king-size in my guest room. My bed was new.

I hadn't even been thinking about him just then. But there he was.

Now, don't get all freaked out about how as Christians we know there's no such thing as ghosts, about familiar spirits, the trickery of demons, satan appearing as an angel of light, etc. Just let me finish the story, OK?

Wearing jeans and my favorite shirt, stretched out with hands behind his head, he looked…normal. I only hesitated a second, knowing if I needed protection God was there, then climbed onto the bed and laid down with my head on his shoulder. I felt his warmth. He put one arm around me. Dead or not, this felt normal.

We chatted about regular husband and wife stuff though I have no memory of our words. Then we relaxed into silence in the comforting togetherness, but of course there were questions I wanted to ask. The problem was that I had a feeling that once I broached that subject, he'd leave, and I didn't want him to leave. After a few minutes, I asked anyway.

"So, um, how is it you're here? Aren't you supposed to be…dead?"

I felt him shrug. "Yeah…"

And he was gone. I didn't feel my head drop onto the pillow or my arm drop to the mattress — he just wasn't there anymore.

I sighed with regret, and laid there a little longer wishing he'd stayed. Then I got up and went about my day.

For a couple of months, when I thought about it, I'd ask, "What WAS that, Lord?" and I'd try to figure out if I was dreaming, having a vision, or if it was real. I thought of my mom's dream a few nights after burying her dad when her dog was also about to die. Her dad had appeared to her in a dream, dressed in his burial suit, holding her dog. He told her he was bringing the dog back to her. And the next morning her dog woke up healed. She knew it was a dream, though we don't know if it was my grandfather, an angel appearing as him, or Jesus appearing as him. The Bible tells of several times Jesus appeared, and referred to Him as an angel of the Lord or something along those lines.

But I was ninety-five percent sure Kevin had not been a dream. Then was it a vision? I felt his physical body, though. I just didn't know if that qualified as a vision. It certainly wasn't a demon. They come only to kill, steal and destroy — not to heal, not to do something kind.

I thought of that weird day in the first year of widowhood when for hours I felt his face in my right hand — his jawline where it fit into my palm, every hair of his beard tickling the length of my fingers, his chin against the heel of my hand. How strange was that? And yet it was comforting. How do you explain something like that?

If Kevin's visit was real, it went against an awful lot of things I'd been taught. Then again, I knew God was bigger than man knew. But if it WAS real, had that been Kevin, or an angel, or Jesus? Surely God didn't grant furloughs from heaven to spend time with family! It was so confusing.

Then one day, I was telling a friend about it, and suddenly I understood. I still didn't know HOW it came about or WHO it really was, but I knew the WHY.

My broken heart was healed. Sure I'd love to have him back, but I was OK. At the moment I made the decision to ask the question, knowing it would likely cause him to leave, I had proven that I was OK. Kevin's "presence" was God showing me that I could do life without Kevin now, and be OK.

Blessed are you who weep now, for you will laugh.
 – Luke 6:21 NRSV

– 8 –

INEXPLICABLE HAPPENINGS
There's No Such Thing as Coincidence

> Coincidence is God's way of remaining anonymous.
> - often attributed to Albert Einstein

> Coincidences mean you're on the right path.
> - Simon Van Booy

> Coincidences are spiritual puns.
> - G.K. Chesterton

Well, no, they're not inexplicable, after all. The explanation is God's love.

Proof of God's Will

> And we know that for those who love God all things work together for good, for those who are called according to his purpose.
> - Romans 8:28 ESV

> The lot is cast into the lap, but its every decision is from the Lord.
> - Proverbs 16:33 ESV

For from him and through him and to him are all things. To him be glory forever. Amen.
- Romans 11:36 ESV

Every good and perfect gift is from above, coming down from the Father of the heavenly lights, with whom there is no change or shifting shadow.
- James 1:17 BSB

GETTING FLEECED

My husband was already living in Canada. Our son and I went back and forth every other month to see him there when he was back from his overseas contracts. It worked, but it was getting tiring. We had purchased a cabin, and Kevin, with our son's help, had gutted it. When my parents visited us, the walls were pink fiberglas insulation and the floors were raw plywood — lovely. But it was coming along. I had done all the space planning, and the tiny cabin lived like it was three times its size. My IKEA catalog was just about worn out, and their cabinetry, paired with my creativity, delivered amazing results.

Our son's room was the smallest, a former storage room. We installed a beautifully handmade elevated bunk. Below it we put a bench with a hinged seat that had come with the place, and added a cushion to make it moderately more comfortable. My brain was working on teenage guy decor ideas, and being in Canada, I immediately thought of Hudson Bay blankets. They're off-white with wide green, red, and dark blue stripes every three feet or so. They hail from back in the days of trading beaver pelts. The problem — they're wool. Why would I give a light-colored wool blanket to a teenage boy? No way was I going to pay that dry-cleaning bill every week. Fleece, one the other hand, is lightweight but warm, never wrinkles, goes through the washer and dryer like a champ, is difficult to stain, lasts forever if it's good quality, doesn't pill, and you don't even have to hem it if you don't want to because it never frays. It's so easy to work with, even I could make simple curtains out of it to go with a couple of blankets. However, I'd had a fleece addiction for a while and had never seen it in the Hudson Bay pattern. I thought, *If I could find some, that would be perfect. Lord, what do you think? Is there any out there?*

When I got back to Georgia, digging around in my stash of decor fabrics (I used to work in that industry), I found a dark blue outdoor fabric that looked woven but wasn't. It was water resistant and had the look of slubs of green and red. Perfect for the bench cushion, and it sure would work well with a Hudson Bay blanket. I picked out a ridiculous bright green paint just for fun. But I still needed the main fabric, and I couldn't get Hudson Bay blankets out of my mind.

A friend who worked in the local textile industry called to tell me the mill was having it's annual pay-by-the-pound fabric sale the next week, and I looked forward to it all weekend. I'd never been before, and when I got there, I have to say, it was disappointing. I found small quantities of several formal fabrics that I picked up for my mother, not even knowing if she could use them in the small cuts they had left. But there was nothing for the cabin. I hated to leave empty-handed and just stood there in the middle of the huge warehouse I'd scoured for two hours secretly hoping for the impossible. Apparently, they didn't even make fleece locally. And in Georgia, how could I ever expect to find a truly Canadian textile pattern? Still, I stood there, eyes roaming all around the perimeter of the huge place on the off chance that from a distance I might see something on a high shelf that I hadn't seen up close. And — nothing.

I turned toward the checkout and nearly tripped, my feet getting tangled up in…fleece. I was standing in a sea of lengths and lengths and lengths of fleece, laying in a tangled mess on the floor in the center of this gargantuan warehouse. If it had been there before, I couldn't have missed it. It was a huge mound. I was surrounded by it! How could I have walked into the mass of it without knowing? And every bit of it was off-white with a green stripe, a red stripe and a dark blue stripe every three feet or so. Hudson Bay blanket fleece — I'd never seen it before and I've never seen it since.

I would have lost heart, unless I had
believed that I would see
the goodness of the Lord in the land of the living.
— Psalm 27:13 NKJV

CROSSING THE LINE

"But the borders are open now!"

"There's open and then there's open. 'A six thousand dollar fine and you'll never get across the border again.' That's what he said — and that's if you even APPROACH the border without up-to-date covid documents. And 'No exceptions,' he said, whether you're American or Canadian."

"Yeah, but that was a Canadian border guard, right? So that would be coming north."

"No, he was U.S. Border Patrol. He was attending a class I was taking, here in Canada."

Wow. That put a damper on the day.

My son, a paramedic, was recounting a conversation from just the week previous. Meanwhile, my childhood friend, Mary, had driven up to his home in Vancouver, Canada, from Seattle that morning to escort me south across the border and get me on a plane to Atlanta. And she had set her work and life up around my travel schedule. It was my birthday. I was going home, and nobody was going to stop me. I had a directive from God, so whose report was I going to believe?

Still, many past experiences made border-crossing, even under perfect circumstances, a matter of some trepidation. Best case, it was a pain. Worst case…well, mid-covid there was really no way of knowing because we were in unprecedented times. I had been turned away from the border once, but under very different circumstances and with no lasting ramifications — I hoped. Plus, Border Services had been known to confiscate the vehicles of those trying to cross illegally…of particular concern since Mary was driving.

She piped up. "I read the newest regulations again this morning, though, and there's a loophole for U.S. citizens…"

"I'm just telling you what one of the enforcers of those regulations told me." Good point. In any situation involving law enforcement, it doesn't really matter in that moment what is lawful, right or just, it only matters what the officer is saying.

Mary began pulling the regs up on her phone, and she was right, but it was definitely in the fine print, and might be subject to interpretation. Arguing regulations with a border agent would at best make for a long night and likely a missed flight. The word 'incarceration' also came to mind.

"There are places you can stop and get tested and vaxxed between here and the border. Or at least there are most days…today is Sunday. Do you want me to make some calls for you?" That was my son's girlfriend.

I considered it for a moment, I must admit. "No, thanks. I know you all think I'm crazy, but I'm not getting vaxxed." And test results would take too long, anyway. I appreciated their not giving me a hard time about it. Over the previous months I think they'd given up changing my mind on that subject. All I needed to know was that in Revelation 18:23, the word 'sorceries' was translated from the Greek word 'pharmakeia' — medicines, Big Pharma. "…All this will happen because your merchants were the nobility of the earth, because all the nations were deceived by your *pharmakeia.*" Who says the Bible isn't relevant today?

I had attended a Bible study months earlier where the leader, when I walked in the door, looked up and said, "Kemala, God is opening a window for you to go home to see your family. I know that's important to you." And weeks before that, she had given me a word from God about a major intersection ahead, and that I had to decide whether to take that turn. Well, today was the day. So, again, whose report was I going to believe?

I was standing on God's…and hoping today was the day that window was open. *Of course it is. TODAY is the day of salvation!*

So I stood by Mary's beautiful RV — an Airstream body on a Mercedes chassis — holding my son for what must have been five full minutes, until they practically forced me into the vehicle. Facing U.S. Border Patrol unvaccinated was nothing compared to leaving my son. Who knew what lay ahead, then, in the middle of covid, him being in the medical field, and with all the crazy Canadian governmental overreach and border closings. I had no idea when I would see him again.

But, God — I knew I was walking out His will for my life. And I knew He had given me that beautiful miracle baby, now 6'2". I had entrusted my son to God's care, so there were good times ahead for us.

I thought about that on the way to the border. Giving my son back to God was practically an act of self defense. When you have a child that flies airplanes and rides Harleys, you simply cannot carry the burden of keeping him safe on your own. It's out of your hands. Only God can do that, and he'd already proven it a few times since KJ started driving and flying. I knew I could trust God in all things.

It was dark, or very near it, when we reached the border. Only one car was in line ahead of us, which was so unlike normal times. I don't remember seeing any other Border Patrol agents — just the one waiting for us to pull forward. We had allowed ninety minutes at the border in our schedule, based on past experience, even Mary's experience that very morning. We found ourselves scrambling to get our passports out before we reached the officer. Mary pushed the button to roll her window down, greeted the handsome young man in uniform, and handed him our documents.

"I live here in Washington State and crossed the border this morning to pick up my friend in Vancouver." I leaned forward so he could see my face clearly to verify my awful passport photo.

"You're an American citizen, too?"

"Yessir." We both started explaining further…"I'm taking her to the airport," Mary added.

"You're both American citizens?"

"Yes, sir. Do you want to see…"

"If you're both citizens, you can go ahead." He handed our passports back through the window. Mary passed them to me. We looked at each other quizzically, more documentation in hand, then both looked back at the officer. What had he just said?

"Sir? Yes, we're both citizens, and we're —"

He gave us an arch look, and an emphatic, "Go!"

Shock.

"Yessir."

"Thank you."

Acceleration.
Deep breaths.
Looking for the exit.
Interstate 5.
Freedom.
Home.

He was not my first border-crossing "angel," but Mary and I both had trouble believing what had just happened.

> For the LORD is our judge; the LORD is our lawgiver; the LORD is our king; he will save us.
> – Isaiah 33:22

IN THE ZONE

There was no reason to take that exit. No signs advertised places to eat or attractions — not even gas stations that I can remember. There were trees, just trees. And even as my son and I pulled to a stop at the top of the ramp and deliberated over which way to turn, there were no businesses or signs in sight, not even cars.

A short distance down the road, after going right, there was an empty parking lot at what looked like a warehouse. It offered an easy turn-around, so I pulled in intending to climb back on the interstate. It was about 3:00 p.m., and the day had suddenly become gray and overcast so that even the trees appeared gray. As I started to turn the wheel in the parking area, we noticed a sign above a partially obscured entrance. Part of that massive building was a guitar store — in the middle of nowhere Pennsylvania.

Guitar was the one thing in my son's life that really inspired him. It had changed his outlook, his attitude, his entire existence at that awkward tween stage when the present is depressing and the future terrifying.

We were on our roundabout way from Georgia to our Canadian west coast island home by way of meeting my husband in Niagara Falls and driving across Canada together. From Atlanta we'd headed due north and stopped near Cincinnati at the amazing Creation Museum. Then we'd headed northeast. I was taking my son to New York City— his first trip there. What do you take a fourteen-year-old boy to see on Broadway? Well, as it happened, Monty Python's Spamalot was playing, so that was a no-brainer. There would be the Statue of Liberty, of course, and Ellis Island to see where one of his great-great-grandfathers had landed. But the main reason we were going to New York was to take him to see Les Paul at the Iridium Jazz Club. I'd heard he often signed autographs after his performances, unless he was just too tired. I was praying for a supernatural boost of energy the night we were there. He was 92.

For those who aren't aware, Les Paul is an icon of the music industry. His wife Mary Ford and he were very popular on the music scene of the 50's and early 60's — before my time — selling millions of records. But much more than that, he was a musical pioneer and renaissance man — a guitarist, songwriter, luthier, and inventor. The solid-body electric guitar, new uses for amplifiers, multi-track recording, dubbing techniques — too many innovations to name — are credited to him. He taught himself to play, became famous for his unique and ever-evolving style, and his influence is obvious in today's music of many genres. He is the only person to be inducted into both the Rock & Roll Hall of Fame (where his is one of the few permanent exhibits) and the National Inventors Hall of Fame. He started out in country music and ended his career with bi-weekly performances at the Iridium Jazz Club — "with adoring metalheads in the audience," as Rolling Stone put it* — right up until his death at age 94. Today, those guitarists who don't bother to learn a little music history still know his name because of a very popular style of guitar named for and designed by him, which is built primarily by Gibson.

So we found ourselves in a remote area, face to face with a guitar store that seemed to appear out of nowhere, doubting it was open based on the empty parking lot — but if it was open, would it be manned by Rod Serling? I parked, and we just stared at each other for a moment.

"Well, if it's open, it's as good a place as any to stretch our legs."

Inside, it was paradise for a teenage guitarist. The feeling of gray from outside lifted. This was the largest, coolest selection of guitars we'd ever seen. Every shape you could imagine, with amazingly funky and artistic paint jobs. And then there were the ones featuring gorgeous woods with gleaming finishes. Some were breathtakingly beautiful. Surely Eddie van Halen shopped here.

After I'd looked around a while I leaned on the counter and enjoyed watching my son in his element. He was enthralled. The counter was built around three sides of a caged area located in the middle of the store. I could see it contained a workshop. One of the two men there asked if I had a question about a guitar, and we began to chat.

---

* Rolling Stone "100 Greatest Guitarists" list online December 18, 2015

"Yes, we're just passing through...just happened to stop... headed to see Les Pau..."

"Les Paul! Lucky kid. Les puts on quite a show. You know he'll sign your boy's guitar after the show — does he have it with him?"

And so I explained the discussion KJ and I had been having in the car. As much as my talented and budding guitarist looked forward to the possibility of meeting the man, the legend, the hero, he was feeling a little trepidation. He wanted Les Paul to sign his Les Paul, but he had just about talked himself into leaving his guitar in the car when we went into the dinner club, for two reasons. His Les Paul was not made by Gibson — it was a less expensive Epiphone. He felt almost as if he was presenting a knock-off to a designer for a signature. Also, it was a vintage guitar, and he hadn't been able to find replacement tuning pegs of the correct age. He didn't want Les Paul to see his guitar in what he considered a state of disrepair, as if he didn't care about it. He could have put in new pegs, but that wasn't good enough — he insisted on authenticity. I knew my child had been scouring the internet for the parts for weeks, but Mr. Paul wouldn't know it. I had silently prayed for a solution. To travel so far, and then to feel embarrassed and not get his guitar signed — he'd regret it all his life.

"Hey, kid! Show me your guitar."

Thirty minutes later, my son's guitar was ready for it's close-up. Just for the joy it gave them to encourage a young musician, the two men had dug out the vintage parts from their overflowing inventory and given KJ's Les Paul a good going over so he could enthusiastically ask it's namesake to sign it. We returned to the car, shaking our heads, still feeling as if we were in the Twilight Zone. It was nearly dark, and we drove ten or more miles down the interstate before finding food and gas. To this day, the entire incident still has a fuzzy, ethereal quality — inexplicable.

What a show it was — worth every one of those 900 miles. Les shared fascinating reminiscences and joked with his band and the audience. How those gnarled, arthritic fingers could move that fast I will never understand. Technical perfection and inspired style — what a combination.

We were near the front of the line for autographs and a moment with the man. Les Paul's son was standing nearby and spoke to me. I mentioned that KJ was a little embarrassed that his Les Paul was an Epiphone. "Why? Daddy's first guitar was an Epiphone."

KJ's turn came, and he laid his guitar in the hands of its creator. My heart nearly exploded with joy when my son heard Les Paul say, "Ahhh, now THAT'S a pretty guitar."

Oh, give thanks to the Lord, for He is good!
For His mercy endures forever.
1 Chronicles 16:34

THE ANGEL OF INTERIOR DESIGN

The main floor of our turn-of-the-century raised cottage, which we would live primarily on, was nearing the finish line. Paint colors were chosen for the plaster walls of most of the ten spacious rooms on that level. The original narrow plank Arkansas pine floors had been refinished and were gleaming. The trim and ceilings were painted, cabinetry, too. But there was something missing…a feeling of intimacy and welcome…wallpaper!

Budgets being what they are, my husband said we could paper one room. So, naturally, I searched out papers for four, and three of those rooms required massive amounts of wallpaper. Not only were the rooms quite large, the walls were twelve feet high. Have I mentioned that budgets aren't really my thing? But for varying reasons, those particular rooms needed the warmth and personality that wallpaper could provide. Having worked on several houses together already, Kevin knew that the final product was going to make it all worthwhile. So, wallpaper it was.

I slaved for days, weeks even, over heavy wallpaper books, page after page, colorway after colorway. I traveled to nearby cities to drag more books home. Truly, I must have looked at a thousand designs. Decor was not something I took lightly in those days. I found an elegant tropical leaf print in light neutrals for the foyer, a colonial trellis pattern in light corals on white for the front room, and a pattern with matching fabric that would camouflage the mid-century pink tile in the downstairs bath. But the kitchen/breakfast room look was elusive.

So there was yet another load of wallpaper books to be returned, another load to be checked out and pored over. then again…then again…and there it was. Not my expected style, but somehow I knew it was perfect.

It was floral, but hovered somewhere between traditional and woodsy. It was fairly dark, though, having a mocha background color, which echoed the painted family room and hall walls. What made this paper special was the dark fern-y silhouettes between the foreground of leaves and pinkish purple-y flowers and the mocha ground…they gave a sense of depth. You were looking into woods or a deep garden border. Although the room was quite large, with a good bit of natural light, it didn't have the high ceilings, so I was trying to convince myself it could handle the darker overall look.

"It's striking, but way too dark. What other colorways does it come in?" That was my mom. And she maintained that viewpoint, which I could agree with in principle, until the day I placed the order for fourteen double rolls of that wallpaper…in off-white background, with the same beautiful soft greens in the leaves, but blue and golden blossoms. The fern fronds were beige. It still tied in with the home's colors of mocha and pale butter, with some light blues in the front. The colorway was attractive, I knew it would be pretty, just more traditional, more expected, less dramatic than the mocha colorway. But it would be bright and hopefully make the room look as large as possible. It had been an agonizing decision, but Mom usually knew what she was talking about.

Shipment seemed to be delayed. I felt it was taking forever to arrive. Two weeks is a long time to bite your fingernails, even figuratively. Finally the heavy rectangular box appeared on the front porch. I dragged it inside and raised the blade of my boxcutter to be sure not to slice into a roll of wallpaper. Finally I'd be able to unroll a length of this paper to see if I really could fall in love with it, or if I'd have to start all over in my search for a paper grand enough for this gorgeous home but with a fresh, young look.

I phoned my mom to come over and see the paper she'd picked out. I knew she'd drop what she was doing, so I'd only have to wait ten minutes — she loved decorating as much as I did. I'd left the box open with all the rolls inside, so she quickly pulled out the roll I'd already removed the plastic covering from.

"I thought…"

"I did. I ordered the soft white background."

She stood there with her mouth open, holding a roll of mocha floral wallpaper — the one I'd originally chosen. I laid the roll against the baseboard and swept the length of paper up the wall, alongside the wide, white-painted, hundred-year-old door frame.

It was gorgeous.

"I guess you're not calling the company to tell them they sent the wrong colorway?"

"Not a chance. Looks to me like God's decorator intervened."

"It does. And it looks like he knows what he's doing."

Papering began in earnest, and when it was completed, that room looked larger than ever, due to the wallpaper's illusion of depth.

I put a swivel club chair in some available space between the kitchen and breakfast area, for Kevin to relax in while I cooked dinner, or vice versa. We enjoyed the chance to talk instead of being in separate rooms in the evening. But at some point in most every day, you'd find me in that cushy chair, just staring at the walls, enjoying the beauty God had provided.

After all, every house has a builder,
but the builder of everything is God.
– Hebrews 3:4 GWT

EVER PRESENT HELP

I think I'd like one of those little drying racks with clips to hold smaller items, one that hooks over a closet or shower rod like a hanger. That would work nicely. I was doing laundry in my new house, appraising my new drying closet and how well the floor plan I'd designed worked.

You know something else I'd like? Some of those clear chair leg caps with the sliders on the bottom to protect the new floor. I like those I saw on TV because they slip right over the chair legs so they don't have to be nailed in, and they're clear, so they don't mess up the decor. When I have a few dollars I don't mind spending on silly little things…

Looking back, I'm not even sure if I was specifically talking to God. And I didn't even write these items on a list. I never mentioned them again. It was just a little wish.

The next time I was in Home Depot, I was disappointed that I wasn't finding what I needed. I wasn't enjoying being there alone, and I felt aimless. Leaving empty-handed felt like I'd wasted half the day, but I had so little in my cart — a magazine — that I questioned if it was worth waiting in line. So I wandered into the tool department, knowing that if Kevin had been with me we would have gone there to "window shop" or to look for a Christmas gift for our son — we liked to give him some kind of tool every year to build up his "arsenal."

So I lingered over tools in a melancholy mood, not finding anything even interesting. Let me reiterate — I was at Home Depot of all places, and in the TOOL department. And why did I look on the backside of a display that had nothing interesting in it? I don't know.

But there, at 75% off and 90% off, was the exact expanding clothes pin hanger I wanted and the As-Seen-on-TV floor protectors.

What kind of God does that?!

The kind that wants you to know that He hears you, that He wants to be involved in your everyday life, and that what's important to you is important to Him. Even when there are starving children in Africa, He wants you to know that He cares about your little First

World wishlist. His riches are for all His kids, and you can't reduce, by your selfish-sounding requests, the supply to others of His abundance of love, provision, prosperity or attention. He's too big. It can't be done. He is yours 24/7/365, just as you are His. Now honor Him with your life, a living sacrifice, in gratitude for His love and grace. That's how it is supposed to work.

> Are not five sparrows sold for two pennies?
> And not one of them is forgotten before God.
> – Luke 12:6 ESV

SWEET

How do I taste You, Lord? I was in Sunday morning service, my pastor was mid-sermon and mentioned Psalm 34:8 — Taste and see that the Lord is good.

I get hearing You, and feeling You, as in sensing Your presence. I use the word 'seeing' when I'm focused on You. But TASTING You? That doesn't even make sense to me.

By the time the pastor finished, I'd engaged with the sermon deeply enough to forget about tasting God. Calling for a special time of prayer, those who wanted were invited to make their way to the altar. So I went down front to pray. I don't remember what my prayer was intended to be about, because as I bowed my head, a soft sweetness touched the center of my tongue and began to grow.

About five years earlier, I'd spent a couple of months in the Philippines, and a congresswoman, with whom I shared the friendship of a local news cameraman, had sent me some of her home grown, tree-ripened mangoes. There are no words to describe the flavor. I wanted to fill a bathtub with little cubes of the soft, silky, juicy, aromatic flesh, and soak in it so that it filled my senses as well as my mouth.

That Sunday, the captivating flavor in answer to the question I'd posed to the Father, was even more exquisite. It blossomed on my tongue, and without parting my lips I opened my jaws, trying to make room for more. I remember a physical sensation, as if it had the shape of my mouth, but it was as light as air. And it grew, involving my cheeks, upper throat, sinus area. The taste was similar to those mangoes — sweet and fruity — but somehow even more sublime. It was fresh and invigorating while being rich and soothing.

Areas of the tongue have taste buds designed for different types of flavors — salty, sweet, bitter, sour and savory. But my mouth was so enmeshed with this deliciousness that my entirety could have been one single receptor designed just for this specific flavor sensation. The taste was intriguing and revelatory at the same time. I could not pray, except to proclaim to God His goodness and of how delightful and delicious He tasted — silently, of course, lest a single atom of flavor escape my mouth. His flavor proved and expressed His goodness, His bounty, His kindness, His exceptional and infinite love. I cannot say how long it stayed, only that as it faded, I screamed inside, *No, no, no, no, don't go, don't go, don't go!* I would have been happy to never eat again, had it remained.

> How sweet are your words to my taste,
> sweeter than honey to my mouth!
> – Psalm 119:103

SHE WILL REACH MANY

In 2019, I was in the thick of writing Disarming Deadly Doctrines, the first book in the Head-Smacker Series, when I traveled to Colorado Springs for the annual Healing is Here Conference at Charis Bible College. It was awesome. Many people were healed — over a thousand the first night — and a baby who died there was raised from the dead.

The second night, I had chosen seats for my friend and myself, and we happened to be surrounded mostly by women. We were all introducing ourselves, chatting, everyone excited and looking forward to the next session starting, when the woman I'd just greeted started praying over me. Let's call her Charity. It was a lovely prayer, but just when I started to feel there was a special word from God about to be spoken, she ended the prayer. We talked a bit more. I liked her very much, but I had that nagging feeling I'd missed out on something. Another person joined our conversation, and I explained that the dear friend I was sitting with I had just met in person! We'd been in touch by phone regularly for months because we were accountability partners in our online book-writing class.

Suddenly, Charity got excited. "You're writing a book?"

"Yes, we both are," indicating my friend who was in a different cluster of ladies.

"Now I understand."

I knew it was the word I'd felt coming forth. "Understand what?"

"When I was praying for you, I heard, 'She will reach many people,' but I didn't say it because it didn't make sense to me."

Say it. Just say it. It doesn't have to make sense to you. If it's from God, it will make sense to the person on the receiving end. You don't have to nail it, especially if it's a gift that's new to you, and it's OK to preface the word with, "Does this make sense to you? I feel like I'm hearing…" But say it.

You may not think of words from God as miracles, and you'd be right. But if you've never been on the receiving end of a word spoken in due season, directly from heaven, you'll feel like you just received a miracle when you do. Suddenly, all is right with the world.

That one word over me provided the endurance to get that book finished and to market. It gave me joy and assured me that I was in God's will, that He was with me in this huge undertaking. And it confirmed the book would accomplish the purpose for which it was written. What had made no sense to Charity made all the difference to me.

...for the Holy Spirit will teach you in that very hour what you ought to say.
– Luke 12:12 NASB

– 9 –

MIRACLES JUST FOR YOU
Expect Them, Receive Them

On the cover of this book I posed the question, "How many miracles is one person allowed?" The answer: as many as one needs, and all that one asks for.

> For all of God's promises have been fulfilled in Christ with a resounding "Yes!" And through Christ, our "Amen" (which means "Yes") ascends to God for his glory.
> - 2 Corinthians 1:20 NLT

> And I will do whatever you ask for in my name, so that the Father's glory will be shown through the Son.
> - John 4:13 GNT

> He that spared not his own Son, but delivered him up for us all, how shall he not with him also freely give us all things?
> - Romans 8:32 KJV

I cannot stress enough that God wants to be part of your life, to provide for you and care for you. It is His nature. Invite Him in and let Him be God in your very own everyday. Put on your expectation. He will not disappoint you.

In order to expect great things, you must first believe that God is capable of great things. It boggles my mind when Christians don't think God can accomplish certain things — heal certain cancers, turn a nation around, raise the dead today. He created everything you see and everything you can't see. What is impossible for Him?

> The LORD considers that an easy thing to do...
> - 2 Kings 3:18 GWT

> "Behold, I am the Lord, the God of all flesh. Is anything too hard for me?
> - Jeremiah 32:27 ESV

In order to expect great things, you must believe that His will is to provide great things. Examine the scriptures. He says the blessings of Abraham are for those who believe. Look up those blessings — you'll be amazed.

> But if I do his work, believe in the evidence of the miraculous works I have done, even if you don't believe me. Then you will know and understand that the Father is in me, and I am in the Father."
> - John 10:38 NLT

> You are the God who performs miracles; you display your power among the peoples.
> - Psalm 77:14 NIV

In order to expect great things, you must believe that He wants to provide these great things for YOU. Look at Adam and Eve. Everything God created for them was for you. Look at every place Jesus shed his blood. There was a purpose for every drop, and every drop provided something great for you. (Isaiah 53:3-12).

> I alone know the plans I have for you, plans to bring you prosperity and not disaster, plans to bring about the future you hope for.
> - Jeremiah 29:11 GNT

Peter said in Acts 10:34, "Truly I understand that God shows no partiality." In other words, if He did it for Adam and Eve, He'll do it for me. And if He does it for me, He'll do it for you. Start expecting. I continue to expect and He continues to supply in amazing ways.

Make no mistake, though — God is worthy of our worship, thanksgiving and awe even when things are not going well, because of Who He is. Don't fall into the trap of praising Him only when you can see that He's working on your behalf. And don't forget that He's working all the time if you're resting in His care, whether you see it in the physical realm yet or not. Praise Him always, because He is always with you and always for you. He has already performed the greatest miracle of all for you if you are saved.

— & —

Here's something most Christians have not been taught. Scripture tells us that angels harken to the voice of the Word of God.

> Bless the LORD, ye his angels, that excel in strength, that do his commandments, hearkening unto the voice of his word.
>
> - Psalm 103:20 KJV

The Word of God has a voice? Yes, it does — your voice! When you put voice to the Word, speaking the scriptures aloud or speaking words that agree with God's, your angels jump into action on your behalf. They respond to God's Word. When your speech runs counter to God's Will for your life — "I knew it, the lab tests came back bad…", "My feet are killing me", "I don't know how we'll make it through the month…" — you're tying their hands. But when you say, "I don't care what the report says, praise God, by Jesus' stripes I am healed!", "Thank you, Lord, for that parking space so close to the door", and "I don't know how we'll make it through the month, but God does, He supplies us according to HIS riches in glory by Christ Jesus." Then, mighty angelic warriors are loosed to defeat those who come to kill you, steal from you and destroy you. So change the way you think of God's promises. Take back the negative words you have spoken all your life, and replace them with God's words.

— & —

God has one kind of power and one kind only. It doesn't matter whether your current problem is physical, mental, emotional, financial, relational, mechanical, spiritual, or one of imminent danger. His one kind of power is every answer to every circumstance. It is the dunamis (miracle-working power – where we get the word *dynamite*) that the Holy Spirit contains inside you and is ready to pour out from an infinite supply on your behalf. That power is LIFE — life poured into your physical body, life for your bank account, life to your marriage, to your womb, to your friendships. He'll speak life over your vehicle, your appliances, your memory, your business, your spiritual growth, your garden, your dreams, your pets and livestock. You saw this in every miracle in my life that you read about. He IS life, He gives life. It's all He is and has for you. He wants to fill your life with His. Let Him. Expect Him to. He WILL.

— & —

There is so much more that I want to say. I could write an entire book on renewing your mind to the word of God; I could explain further about God being no respecter of persons; I long to expound on everything Jesus bought for you on His journey from the Garden of Gethsemane to His resurrection. And, oh my goodness, I want to tackle the subject of our words, even though I am far from conquering my own mouth. But when you boil it all down, it's really just about trust — trusting the Lord with your life.

I have confidence in God's grace toward me. I do not live from miracle to miracle, I simply trust God. The miracles are just a result of God's promises coming to pass in my life. I don't look for miracles, they just find me. He wants to do the same for you.

> All these blessings will come and overtake you, because you obey the LORD your God.
> - Dueternomy 28:2 CSB

They will chase you down! Rest in Him, so they can catch up.

```
And the same God who takes care of me will
supply all your needs from His glorious riches,
which have been given to us in Christ Jesus.
         - Philippians 4:19 N LT
```

GLOSSARY OF BIBLE TRANSLATIONS

It is the glory of God to conceal a thing: but the honour of kings is to search out a matter.
— Proverbs 25:2 KJV

AMP and **AMPC** - Amplified Bible and Amplified Bible Classic Edition
Scripture quotations taken from the Amplified® Bible (AMP), Copyright © 2015 by The Lockman Foundation
Used by permission. www.Lockman.org
Scripture quotations taken from the Amplified® Bible (AMPC), Copyright © 1954, 1958, 1962, 1964, 1965, 1987 by The Lockman Foundation
Used by permission. www.Lockman.org

ASV - American Standard Version (public domain)

BSB - Berean Standard Bible
The Holy Bible, Berean Standard Bible, BSB
Copyright ©2016, 2018 by Bible Hub
Used by Permission. All Rights Reserved Worldwide.

CSB - Christian Standard Bible
Scripture quotations marked CSB have been taken from the Christian Standard Bible®, Copyright © 2017 by Holman Bible Publishers. Used by permission. Christian Standard Bible®, and CSB® are federally registered trademarks of Holman Bible Publishers

ESV - English Standard Version
Scripture quotations marked ESV are from the ESV® Bible (The Holy Bible, English Standard Version®), copyright© 2001 by Crossway Bibles, a publishing ministry of Good News Publishers. Used by permission. All rights reserved.

GNT - The Good News Translation
Scripture quotations marked (GNT) are from the Good News Translation in Today's English Version- Second Edition Copyright © 1992 by American Bible Society. Used by Permission.

GWT - God's Word Translation
GOD'S WORD is a copyrighted work of God's Word to the Nations. Quotations are used by permission. Copyright© 1995 by God's Word to the Nations. All rights reserved.

KJV - King James Version (public domain)

NASB - New American Standard Bible
Scripture quotations taken from the New American Standard Bible (NASB),
Copyright © 1960, 1962, 1963, 1968, 1971, 1972, 1973,
1975, 1977, 1995 by The Lockman Foundation
Used by permission. www.Lockman.org

NIV - New International Version
THE HOLY BIBLE, NEW INTERNATIONAL VERSION®, NIV® Copyright © 1973, 1978, 1984, 2011 by Biblica, Inc.™ Used by permission. All rights reserved worldwide.

NLT - New Living Translation
Holy Bible, New Living Translation, copyright © 1996, 2004, 2015 by Tyndale House Foundation. Used by permission of Tyndale House Publishers, Inc., Carol Stream, Illinois 60188. All rights reserved.

NKJV - New King James Version
Scripture taken from the New King James Version®. Copyright © 1982 by Thomas Nelson. Used by permission. All rights reserved.

NRSV - New Revised Standard Version
Scripture taken from the New Revised Standard Version Bible, copyright © 1989 National Council of the Churches of Christ in the United States of America. Used by permission. All rights reserved worldwide.

Made in the USA
Columbia, SC
04 April 2025